SUSPICIOUS CIRCUMSTANCES –
AN ALBUM OF EVENTS AND ODDITIES WITH
THOUGHTS ON THE WORD WHAT

A. ROBERT LEE

SUSPICIOUS CIRCUMSTANCES –
AN ALBUM OF EVENTS AND ODDITIES WITH THOUGHTS ON THE WORD WHAT

 **EYEWEAR** PUBLISHING

First published in 2020
by Eyewear Publishing Ltd
Suite 333, 19-21 Crawford Street
Marylebone, London W1H 1PJ
United Kingdom

Graphic design and typeset by Edwin Smet
Cover painting by Masumi Sato
Author photograph by Josefa Vivancos-Hernández

The right of A. Robert Lee to be identified as author of
this work has been asserted in accordance with section 77
of the Copyright, Designs and Patents Act 1988
ISBN 978-1-913606-06-0

WWW.EYEWEARPUBLISHING.COM

For at least a dozen fellow suspects:

Richard Berengarten (Cambridge)
Rex Burns (Denver)
Roberta Eel (UN)
Frida Forsgren (Kristiansand)
Mark Gresham (Tokyo)
Jared Lubarsky (Barcelona)
Deborah Madsen (Geneva)
Peggy Pacini (Paris)
Tino Villanueva (Boston)
Te-Hsing Shan (Taipei)
Bent Sørensen (Harup Thy)
Cathy Waegner (Siegen)
Robert Yeo (Singapore)

TABLE OF CONTENTS

SUSPICIOUS CIRCUMSTANCES

WHAT?

Suspicion all our lives shall be stuck full of eyes.
— Shakespeare, *Henry IV, Part I*

A minute examination of the circumstances served only to make the case more complex.
— Arthur Conan Doyle, 'The Adventure of the Empty House'

Wherever you go, there you are.
— Quentin Crisp

NO SUSPICIOUS CIRCUMSTANCES

No suspicious circumstances? You have to be kidding.

Pretty well all circumstances, you suspect, are, well,
suspicious. Even when found otherwise. Especially when
found otherwise.

Court cases give you suspects every hour on the hour.

I suspect everyone and I suspect no one. So speaks the
detective sage, Inspector Clouseau, clad in Peter Sellers
French accent.

Not the only gumshoe to take that view.

Sherlock, Philip Marlowe, Miss Marple, Inspector
Maigret and Judge Dee join the suspecters.

Haven't you yourself more than a few times grown
greatly suspicious? Haven't you, conversely, confessed to
never having suspected?

Lost items, keys and clothing especially, make the
reckoning. A number of suspicions gather around
personal upsets, whether brought on by something you
did or didn't. Or someone else did. Or did not.

Deaths have to rate high. As do most murders.

There have been all those suspicious offers, types,
packages, goods, characters, foodstuffs, and always a
prime worry, reasons. Your life has never been entirely
free of suspicious smells, floorboards, news, water or

gas leaks, neighbours, meteorological forecasts, not to mention intentions. A thousand novels, *Tom Jones* not least, turn on suspect births.

Time of course enters the process. It seems you were forming suspicions long ago. Or just some time back. Or right now as yet more have come into play. The current suspicions raise another question. How often do you go into suspicion-mode or is it just once in a while?

Suspicions come your way from other pages and screens. What about all those dark suspicions in Greek drama? Or *Othello*? Then there are the headlines bringing news of a latest plane crash or bank scandal. You might call to mind the plotline in John Buchan's *The Thirty-Nine Steps,* all World War I espionage and a suspect on the run. Alfred Hitchcock does double duty: Cary Grant as maybe murderer in *Suspicion* and Henry Fonda as the unfairly caught-out musician in *The Wrong Man.*

Time and again, in a variety of situations, you think a suspicious touch of irony is at work. I dare hardly mention the times you have misconstrued.

Of course, or so you say, much of it has to do with circumstances. Starting, exactly, with those circumstances of birth.

Plus each of the others.

Special circumstances. Changed circumstances. Reduced circumstances.

Do you remember when circumstances didn't permit?

Or when it was a case of circumstances, like the weather, permitting?

You have taken refuge in mitigating or even aggravating circumstances. You have been privy to both fortunate and unfortunate sets of circumstances. There have been times when, judiciousness itself, you have heard yourself saying *in the circumstances*. Other times there's been the reverse swing into *under no circumstances*.

It isn't as if you haven't suspected yourself of daydreaming, this way or that, in matters of circumstance.

It could have been while hearing Elgar's *Pomp and Circumstance*.

It could have been amid some mental dawdling when you started to think of spin-off film and book titles:

> James Ellroy, *L.A. Circumstantial*
> Jane Austen, *Clive and Circumstance*
> Herman Melville, *The Circumstance-Man*

Suspicions and circumstances often search out each other.

The circumstances are suspicious says the Chair of the Enquiry, the Fraud Squad, the newspaper editorial.

A suspicion arises that evidence about the circumstances has been tampered with.

I suspect you don't really know the circumstances.

Circumstantial? I suspect so.

But you keep on enquiring.

Birth and Death. Light and Dark.

Under no circumstances? Under all of them.

No suspicious circumstances? You have to suspect.

No suspicious circumstances? The most suspicious thing of all.

VULTURE WORK

Years back, when my body had the chutzpah to think it could manage a twice-a-week squash game, I was briefly partnered on court with a student from India. We were all yellow spot ball, re-strung racquets, even on-court white shorts and shirt. Lots of drop-shots and second serves. Let would be duly called, and score-lines went up and down from 9-7 to 9-0. American squash scoring I had learned was a tad different.

His family was from Bombay, a Parsi business dynasty, who with an eye to future inheritance had sent their son to acquire a degree in Accountancy at a UK university. Impeccable upper-class Indian English in speech, a whizz on the court. He and I took to changing-room chats about everything from the Raj to latest cricket.

Over time he revealed more of his life and destiny. At one time the family had him marked for possible future Parsi priesthood. He knew his Zoroastrian scripts and rites and could not but have been more fully cognizant of the history that had brought Parsi refugees from Muslim Persia to Gujarat and especially the trade city of Surat – not to mention Mumbai and Karachi. Little did I know then that Freddie Mercury, Queen's rock-opera's voice supreme, would come of Parsi stock. I'd also once seen Zubin Mehta, another Parsi, wielding the conductor's baton. Later, reading Salmon Rushdie's *The Ground Beneath Her Feet*, there was Ormus Cama, this time a fictive Parsi rock star.

It was a bonus to learn more from my squash theologian. He explained about the prophet Zarathustra – which,

like most, I knew of principally as being nestled inside
the title of Nietzsche's half-impossible philosophy
and Strauss's music which would come round again
in Kubrick's *2001: A Space Odyssey*. We touched on the
Holy Book, the *Avesta*, and on the role of Fire in the
Cosmos's Good and Evil warfare. I also heard for the first
time about Ahura Mazda, the religion's Creator God.
Hitherto the only time I'd met the word Mazda was in
a local shop selling lightbulbs, a trademark name used
first by General Electric in 1909. Years later, in Chicago,
I found myself driving a Mazda rotary engine car, the
product of a Japanese company founded of all places in
Hiroshima in 1920.

Further après-shower chat brought us on to the Farsi,
or Parsi, language, and its role inside so much Hindi-
speaking India. It also led to word about the various
festivals and calendar observances. Of relevant note,
too, was what he had to say about Fire Temples, the
ever-burning flame of life. The largest gathering of these
was to be found in Mumbai but one was to be seen in
nowhere more exotic than south London.

Which brought us on to death. Another kind of temple.
Namely Temples of Silence. Funerary Parsi practice, at
least of a traditional kind, requires that bodies be placed
on a downward sloping platform, be left exposed, and
then given to the city vultures to strip down to the bones
– they, in turn, to be deposited in a sand and charcoal
well. After three days the soul then makes its way across
the Chinvat Bridge between the present world and the
next and, having crossed, rises to Heaven or plunges to
Hell. All depending on whether the deceased has led the
Good or Bad life. Christians, relative newcomers given
Zororastrians were out and about some eight centuries
previous, might find some of this familiar.

As to them there vultures...

Long after my squash days, and long after having lost
touch with my informant, they made another bow. I
was TV-surfing. Up popped a Nature documentary, one
of those between-the-news or favourite films. National
Geographic or a programme whispered into being by
David Attenborough, he to whom every stick insect or
jaguar or puffin is a familiar. But this time it was your
hook-beak, wattled neck and peck your eyes out vulture.

What I learned then, and followed up with some
internet and book research, was that vultures can go
at dead flesh and all attendant offal and gut because
of powerful digestive stomach acids. They can ingest
virtually anything because said acids kill any lurking
bochilli, among them anthrax. Kind of all-purpose
demolition units. Clean-up scavenger artists.

However, this brings us back to our squash colloquia.
My partner paused and with not a little mournfulness
summoned memories of Mumbai and elsewhere. *We are
now suffering*, he said, *VULTURE SHORTAGE*. Rare,
you'll agree, even for the language of complaint.

It turns out that cow corpses, those given Hindu
reverence and to which vultures have resource also,
contain Diclofenos. This, a species of cyanide, has
worked its toxic effect on all vultures. In the last ten
years, it appears, there has been an over-90% drop in the
vulture population. However, word is out, something of
a comeback is being staged. Numbers, if marginally, are
on the rise.

Which will be good news for the Parsi dead. They can rid themselves of bodily corruption and head for the afterlife secure that tradition has been respected.

But the issue stays in the memory. I mean you have heard of any number of shortages. Size 7 shoes maybe. Spare roof tiles. Clotted cream. Hosepipe clips. No plumbers when you want them.

But VULTURE SHORTAGE has to take its place of honour in the thesauri (or is that thesauruses?) of catchphrase.

It's worthy.

TEETH BARED

There has never, it seems, been a shortage of shop and franchise mascots. Most city streets once vaunted a swirling barber's pole. Restaurants have long had their smiling, usually French-aproned waiter manikins, often with menu attached. Butchers continue to display a frolicking lamb, a resigned bullock. Dickens and co. have kept you mindful of the pawnbroker's three balls sign.

Latterly it has been Ronald McDonald, red and yellow clown in white-face smile beckoning you to burgers and extra fries and with a Coke or Pepsi to wash them down. You can find top-hatted Mr. Peanut, plus monocle and cane. Every city has its Colonel, of course, KFC's Southern plantation 'goodwill' gent duly accoutred in goatee and western bow tie.

Think, too, of all those ice-cream parlours, hotdog stands, clothes-store figures, fish eateries with smiling lobster or compliant trout. And never least in my own viewing, a giant alabaster cow to be seen, even petted, as advertizing icon for frozen yogurt.

Which brings us to Japan, my own base for over a dozen years.

And teeth.

Not the least of my longtime academic stay in Tokyo was getting the body-basics sorted out. You might have been lucky and alighted upon a semi-English-speaking eye specialist or podiatrist. You might have chanced your own baby Japanese grammar and tackled a local physiologist for a bout of bursitis or ligament trouble. On one occasion, having been afflicted with the usual Spring sinusitis, nasal drip included, I was referred to a rhinologist who spoke fondly of his recent holiday in New Mexico before discovering I was from the UK. An annual medical, required by my employer, had me trying to say in elementary Japanese that I had forgotten to bring a sample but would be back the following day with the allotted vial.

Not unnaturally among all these features were dentist visits. It was my good fortune to get referred to one who had trained in Brisbane. She would explain in near-perfect Australian English issues of fillings, risks of gingivitis, whether a bridge was necessary, and how best to floss without hitting yourself in the eye. The latter was something I'd long been prone to do, a kind of awkward variation of string theory. The hygienist, however, was a non-English speaker (why should she have been?). So she went about drilling out plaque and the like with silent goodwill although accompanied by the occasional velar grunt from myself.

The office was benign zoo-land. You went in and heard birdsong, an occasional baboon love-call. There was about the place a scent, some eco-perfume which doubtless summoned calm, zen equilibrium. To get into the Chair, true to Japanese etiquette, you had deposited your shoes at the entrance and donned what might be called dental slippers. Once you lay back, bib upon your chest, hands akimbo, a TV screen came into play. So that while your molars were getting theirs you could watch a Japanese soap, or depending on the season, whole slews of baseball.

All of this was presaged by the dentist's advertising icon. Namely a giant wax (or maybe it was plastic) tooth. Seriously large. It held dominion at the foot of the stairway that led to the clinic. It had, as it were, two tooth legs, a slightly bulbous body, and a crown or top that I learned is called occlusal. One time I saw it through a rain-sheet with a touch of fog in the air and thought it looked not a little like an ice-cream cone.

But this was a tooth with attitude.

Seated. Squat.

A mushroom. A marshmallow.

It had that 'we shall not be moved' look about it. A dental Buddha almost. Jabba the Hutt from *Star Wars*. One of C.S Lewis's gnomes in *The Chronicles of Narnia*. Or a goblin in J. K. Rowling's *Harry Potter* books. Stone effigies came to mind. Etruscan. Chinese. Peruvian. Ashanti.

I mean we all have teeth, at least to start with after the usual baby gums. And even those who lose them have the possibility of getting a false set.

So there it stood, indeed still stands.

Gateway to Novocaine and its successor anesthetics. Plus to horizontally viewed TV with due Japanese commentary.

Heraldic emblem of root canal work, periodontal treatment, de-scaling and implants.

It won't make any national art gallery or metropolitan sculpture garden. But it invites its own garland.

Nothing less than a Tooth Oscar.

ANOTHER COUNTRY

We've more or less got used to L.P. Hartley and the another country of the past. And if it's not *The Go-Between*, then there's always James Baldwin's *Another Country* with its Manhattan sex-and-race entanglements.

But then you come up more than a bit short with actual countries that have been made over into yet other countries: those of TV commercial and the travel poster.

You find yourself, by ear or eye or both, set down in virtual geographies, lands of happy hour, jingle, travel sublimity.

It's not hard to compile a list of these near extra-planetary real places. Each a Utopia. Each a Heaven on Earth. Dreamlands. Ultimate destinations.

> *Timeless Macedonia*
> *Remarkable Indonesia*
> *Malaysia, Truly Asia*
> *Happy Trails Texas*
> *Vietnam, Tireless Charm*
> *Incredible India*
> *Key West, Close to Perfect*
> *Australia, A Place in the Sun*
> *From Georgia with Love*
> *Azerbaijan, Land of Fire*
> *Poland Invites You to a Fisherman's Paradise*
> *Skegness, It's So Bracing*
> *Business Friendly Bahrain*
> *I Love Ukraine*
> *Switzerland Invites You*

Ireland is Waiting to Welcome You
Mountaineering Choose France
Santa Fe — Southwestern Dude Ranches
Summer in Wonderful Copenhagen
Le Soleil Toute l'Année sur la Côte D'Azur
New York The Wonder City
Peru of the Incas
Egyptian Pharaohs
Tblisi is Waiting for You

You could add your own plethora. After all, during childhood or lounging on the adult sofa, you have been coming across them all your life.

Maybe, too, you have paused over those that just about hint of something beyond the technicolour. I remember seeing a 1930s poster for Cuba emblazoned with the words *So Near, so Fast* and a more modern one saying *Escape to Cuba*. There's also the ad that doesn't altogether have you imagining Paradise. Pretty enough pastel of Scandinavia but bearing the indisputable truth: *Oslo, Capital of Norway*. Acoustically at least, are you not hearing shades of Hamlet, Prince of Denmark? Or Don Quixote, Man of La Mancha?

The question then becomes: how do you get to any of these places? I mean, sure, you can book a flight, a train, a bus even, to actual Macedonia, actual Copenhagen, even actual India or actual Azerbaijan. But that's not the same.

Those hours in front of the TV, or sidelong glimpses as you sauntered past a Travel Agent's window, have done their magic-carpet seduction. Plus you have this or that ditty ringing in the ears. These have truly become hills

alive with the sound of music. Or the sound of mucus
– as one acerbic wit was known to observe. Whatever
the occasion there you are, Walter Mitty-like, slightly
a-daze, ready in the mind's eye for the off.

Perfect landscape. Perfect weather. Perfect clothes.
Perfect smiles. A destination so bloody perfect that
you might think yourself walking if not flying into
brushstroke nirvana.

Nobody mentions price, the delayed flight, lost luggage,
the brief spat you had with your partner. Nor the slight
quease that came about after the car drive to the airport.
Nor is there mention of unruly kids or the seemingly
lost ticket. Did you get a receipt for the Duty Free?
What happened when you scuffed your shoe and nearly
fell? There's the zip that came loose on the carry-on
luggage. Not to mention the spilled drink. And *Oh
My God did we leave the back door unlocked?* You could go
political and give thought to migrants, traffickers, the
drug trade, disease, or that hardiest of perennials, war.

All very well talking about reality checks, however.
Mid-winter, even a damp Spring, will have you back
at those TV and poster countries. Pleasure domes.
Yourself the holiday swashbuckler. Latter-day da Gama,
Columbus, albeit with travel insurance and motion
sickness pills.

A monarch among voyagers. Bound for modern
paradise.

Plus Value Added Tax.

NIGHT CALL

Lovesick swain. I must have been fourteen, maybe
fifteen, when that phrase first entered my lexical
universe. We were making our bow towards the Bard in
an English class at school and the teacher made reference
to Romeo. I knew nothing then of balconies in Verona
and had never heard a name like Tybalt.

And for sure I'd never come across a Friar. Years on, and
accoutred with a degree in literature, I got so I could
summon blighted love-figures in Shakespeare with the
best of them. Danish Hamlet and Ophelia, Moorish
Othello and Desdemona. I could even manage an extra
Friar or two: Friar Francis in *Much Ado About Nothing* or
Friar Patrick in (where else?) *Two Gentlemen of Verona*.

All of which supplies contextual tracking for the
memory of my own touch of lovesick *swain-age* and star-
crossed woe.

The father of one of my pals worked as head engineer
at the city ice rink. A man who drove an elephantine
plough across the rink once the skaters had wrapped
up for the day. The pal would on occasion have me go
with him and finagle a free pair of boots, blades and
all, so I, too, could glide or pivot. He, of course, was
a positive ace. Spins, jumps, twistles, the odd sprint.
He also usually stayed on the ice after the rest of the
duffers like myself had limped off – music came on and
there he was, with some young female partner, given
over to synchronized dancing. Looking back I realize
it wasn't quite the Olympics. But he knew the moves,
and occasionally attempted one of those lifts that you

see in pairs figure skating. All of it I kind of looked on with envy, often with a wet trouser-seat from each too frequent visitation to the ice surface.

It was then, however, that my career as swain more or less began. Propped up against the barrier after yet another abortive endeavour to enter the skating ranks I fell in with a young woman who, like myself, had little ability to glide. It wasn't all commiseration. Eyes met. A hint of interest from her seemed to flicker. *What chance*, said I, a mini-Montague to her considerably assured Capulet, *we could maybe meet in town the next day*. For the all-purpose 'walk'. Or, a step into the beyond, a film. Clearly bowled over by my Veronese English or ice-skating doublet, she said yes. Thunder. Fortune's fool. Blushing pilgrims.

And so, as much a novice in intimacy as in the three-point turn, I was on my way deep into *swain-age, swain-ery*. And unusual for the times she was willing to let me have a phone number (not all homes had phones in that era – my own certainly didn't). This meant further contact, ear to ear, voice to voice. My own balcony as it were.

In fact it would be better if I did call, just to confirm. Why not?

After a night heavy in anticipation the next day dawned. Pure Italy. An orchard day as it were. It went slower than a sloth's tree-climb. But come early evening there I was at the local phone-box, coins at the ready, number upon paper. In went the small change, the ringing seemed an age. And a male voice answered, clearly her father. Bold as Cock Robin I asked for the girl in person.

The upshot was a pause. A silence. *I'll check*, he said. *Wait a minute*. Impatience was not the half of it. I was also conscious that the money wouldn't let me stay on the line for ever. *No*, he intoned stentoriously, *Nobody here of that name*.

My God, what had I done? Written down the wrong number? Misdialled? Was this my fluffed chance to be in living, breathing Shakespeare?

Receiver in hand I checked, re-checked. It all seemed right. So, courage to the sticking place, I asked if this was my Juliet's father? *Who?* he asked, almost affronted as I couldn't help thinking. *Do you know where you are ringing?* Of course I did.

My own obscure object of desire.

To which, ice-rink riposte to perfection, he said *This is the local crematorium*.

Love in flames. Passions reduced to ashes.

I haven't been to a skating rink since.

NOT THE ONLY CLAPHAM JUNCTION

Jigsaw train stations.

I can't be the only foot passenger who has gone up, down, left, then right, and then back over each one more time, in certain of these big-map rail hubs. You get the Express due on Platform 3a confused with the Medium Express due on Platform 3b four minutes later but the one not stopping at three minor stations.

Given you have to peer, or that your eyes are not as detail-sharp as in earlier years, was it Platform 1 or 11 you thought yours?

Should you be standing to the rear or fore of the lines, a Mondrian geometry of red, blue and yellow-orange with extra numbers circled over each at the platform edge? Which indicates the through train, which the stopping train?

If, too, you are lugging that suitcase, the one with the books and laptop as well as the underwear, how come the lift is always being serviced? And when it works are you sure it's actually moving when there's that moment you think yourself maybe caught in elevator time for all eternity?

And then there's the question of the ticket. Is what you have bought, boldly having taken on the automatic dispenser, the one-day, the three-day, the six-month, or the one usable only between 11am and pre-evening rush hour? Did you get the concessionary rate for age, or infirmity, or because you have opted to travel on a

weekday? As things have turned out you happen to be
en route of a Saturday, off for the weekend. So it may be
extra payment when the Inspector sways down the train
corridor. Not to mention a likely reprimand. Thank
God, you murmur silently, it's not Sunday. That, the
very call-sign of doom, could mean WORKS. Followed
by *A bus service is being provided*.

It doesn't help that not a few of these mega-stations
fuse with the Metro. So from South London to Tokyo's
Shinjuku, or from Berlin's Hauptbahnof to New York's
Penn Station, you can all too easily get your station
arrows muddled. The Exit for this but not quite the Exit
for that. And if, amid the flurry, and for whatever reason
of platform, departure time, ticket or suitcase, you see
the words *Rapid Transit* you may well feel the gods of
rail-track irony are pursuing you with a vengeance. Are
you not semi-marooned, lost in rail space?

I haven't mentioned announcements. It's one thing if
you happen to be in China or Moscow and know that
you won't understand. But when it's your own language,
your own country even, and the tannoy sounds like a
smoker's cough, you know you are in for the equivalent
of rendition. It surely said something that bore a scary
resemblance to the train time and platform you wanted.
Didn't it? I mean there was echo, blur, rumble, and three
teenagers were listening to a boom-box just to your
right. No point in asking fellow passengers themselves
on the edge of breakdown. They didn't hear either. Then
there it is again, just as blurred, but in Estuary French
to show the station was up on the international world.
Together with an admonition to keep your luggage with
you at all times.

Clapham Junction I came to rather late. It is, the information leaflet explains, an Interchange Station. Which maybe also explains the slight snobbery I used to feel towards it. Euston, St. Pancras, Charing Cross, Paddington, Waterloo – these were rail quality, real stations through which you took real trains across fields and distance. All points of the UK compass. North and South, East and West.

But Clapham *Junction?* In Battersea, more or less, where they have the Dogs Home, now known more properly under the full monicker of Dogs and Cats Home. There was also the sound and sight of the very word Clapham. A hint of tacky applause, hands joined in some grudging or sub-standard slap.

Finally, on a wing and prayer, you believe yourself on the right platform. Train due in 5 minutes says the screen. On ascending this stairway, and crossing that overpass, your gaze has just about had time to take in the sheer proliferation of tracks. Metal curve and longitude. Train carriages in a profusion of commercial logos and colours.

You might conjure up the equivalent of a cranial nerve-system. Steel ganglia. Tryons. Electro-networks. But the smell of doner kebab, the sight of a spilled small café latte, get you back to train reality.

And there you are, you and luggage to hand, with the train coming into view. Clapham Junction, or any and all of its rail-cousins, vindicated. Are you not reborn, a train station evangelical?

But where did you put your damned ticket?

FAMILY MELVILLE

Sonoma County. The moment you hear the name your nasal antennae think wine. Or at least wine country. Your Sauvignons and your Cabernets. Your Glen Ellen and Sebastiani. That might well be enough to get the pulse energised, the tasting buds stirred. But, as the Elizabethans were prone to intone: stay. There's more to hand.

Not least, and something that has had shall we say its own vintage association with wine, namely education. In the immediate case a notable Junior College begun in what for settler California was virtually the Tudor Period, 1918. It is there, keeping up Queen Elizabeth I's idiom, to which we now repair.

Like a lot of literary people who get into academia I opted for a writer around whose work there seemed no alternative but to hover, and in well-trodden library-stack manner, to take on a thesis. I speak here of Herman Melville. He of South Seas white whale, a Kafka story like 'Bartleby', and the maybe extra-judicial hanging of the impressed young mariner Billy Budd – to be given film treatment in 1962 by that multilingual actor and virtuoso Russo-Polish Englishman, Peter Ustinov.

And it was about *Moby-Dick* that I had been invited to lecture. An hour or so of American epic to be unleashed upon a student audience. Eyes on the prize as it were. Skateboards all to be parked. The prospect of phrasing like *Call me Ishmael* on every lip.

I'd flown out to Spring California from Winter Chicago. So rather than melting snow sludge, or that intimidating phrase 'Wind Chill Factor', here were leaves of grass, the greenery of tree and plant life. An occasional shower perhaps, the odd wind gust. But a climate in which thermal underwear could be thought of as couture sported only on Uranus or Pluto.

It was also a lift to see the publicity. The college's art department had come up with a diving sperm-whale inside blue-green ocean waters and developed from a Rockwell Kent woodblock done for the 1930 Lakeside edition of the novel. Good company in which to find yourself advertised.

So it was meet and greet after the brief road trip from San Francisco. My host murmured cautions not to go, well, overboard, and indulge too esoteric or academic a run at the text. This indeed, was to be a student audience, and for whom *Moby-Dick* could as easily be dead blubber as any call to imagination.

Lunch with various Faculty people followed. A chat about classes being taught. This aspiring professor's new article, that professor's maybe full-length monograph to be magicked into being. I was cast as the willing ear, the visiting academic cheerleader. And from there it was a guided stride to the classroom where the lecture was to happen. In came the students, some with a genuine nose of interest, others clearly dragooned.

An Introduction had you wondering whether you were truly the person being presented. This publication, that teaching base. And then it came time for the off. 55 minutes of lecture-music if, as promised, you were keeping to time.

Mindful of prior admonition it was a brief gesture towards what makes for literary Epic. Also a nod towards getting through the novel as bulk. Added in were some carefully select examples of word-play and ironic riff on Melville's part.

Your own eye would occasionally look to the assembled audience. Were you hitting the right note? Was that a yawn near the front, a look of distraction in the case of the student sitting near the window? Who had actually read the book? On you went, whatever the might-be dips of attention. The Ancient Mariner. The lecturer with a gleam in his eye.

After which, you hoped, a flourish to round out things. Melville as champion, explorer, cosmologist, pre-postmodern, postmodern, even post-postmodern. Not to say *not* postmodern. Whichever, or switching from Elizabethan to Californian, you might have said whatever.

Applause. More or less. Then a thank you, an invitation to questions or comment. Just two, both from sympathetic Faculty members.

After which we headed out, a walk to one of the college lounges where there'd be a sit-down, coffee, some follow-up nicety and chat.

We were almost there when my host half-blanched, certainly gave way to a frown of concern. A small student group from the lecture were approaching. *Oh my God,* said she, *it's Mel.* Nice name-echo of Melville himself.

The Mel in question was a known quantity among the Faculty, an athlete who apparently could disrupt a class as quickly as he could turn a handstand or score a touchdown. Needless to say, as an Alpha, as pure physique, he was slightly ahead of the rest.

Up he came. No bromides, no how do you do's.

I guess you really like that Melville guy, said he. *How come? Is he a relative of yours?*

Kind of, I wanted to say.

Or perhaps I should have opted for kinda.

GENDER ASSIGNMENT

Oklahoma. Ooook-lahoma. Where the wind comes sweepin' down the plain. Thank you Oscar Hammerstein II, New York librettist and musical teammate of Richard Rogers.

Little did I think, being raised in the industrial North of England, that my focus would one day turn to the Great Plains southwest of the US. And if Manchester has its naming in Roman Latin, Oklahoma, I was to learn, looks to Choctaw etymology of which there was not a lot about in the streets of my boyhood.

But it was in Colorado that I met the brother of a Professorial colleague. He'd been a middle order diplomat. US Foreign Service assignments in Beirut, Minsk, Timişoara (with that cedilla under the s), and sundry other locales vital to the American national interest. He had been raised – how you felt could it have been otherwise? – in rural Oklahoma.

In no time at all he and I got into serious talk. Not, as might first have been expected, about living next to mighty Texas. Or the seams of history that had caused the state-to-be of 1907 initially to have been dubbed Indian Territory. Or dustbowls and panhandles. Or even the human genus that had passed into usage as Okies. Kin to Appalachia's Poor Whites. Rednecks. Depression-era migrants.

There was, too, a whole other Oklahoma gallery. Dorothy Lange's photography. Woodie Guthrie ballads. Will Rogers' storytelling. And always Steinbeck's *Grapes of Wrath*.

But these, equally, were not the centre of our conversation. Far from it. My ex-diplomat had a small landholding, a farm if we were going up-market. Not corn. Not alfalfa. Not dairy. None of the above.

No Sir, we are talking OSTRICHES.

He was a veritable fount of avian information. As befitted a member of the American Ostrich Association, currently headquartered in Tehachapi, California. Even Manchester Latin had not prepared me for the bird's taxonomical posh name: *Struthio Camelus*. Not to be thought some species of Australian curse-phrase.

Ostrich Camel. You can blame that 18th-century Swede, Carl Linnaeus. He of plants, animals and other classification.

We are also talking affinities with emus, kiwis, moas, rheas and the like. They lay eggs that can take up to an hour to cook. Loggers-up of no less than 70 kms per hour. Mature height of more than 2 metres. Adult weight twice that of a grown man. Thermally self-regulating. Largest eye of any vertebrate. Serious gullet, a skin and gristle periscope. Feather cornucopia.

Nor is Oklahoma their only, as it were, neck of the woods. You can make their acquaintance in Somalia, South Africa's Cape Province, parts of the Outback, or even England's Suffolk. You can also attend ostrich races either with or without riders and carriages (try Virginia City, Nevada, or Ellis Park, Kentucky). Injunctions are to be heard cautioning against loss of betting slips.

In a love handles age ostrich steak has become a trend. Is it not recommended by the American Heart Association?

Lean. Can be served as fillet, burger, stew, not to say tenderloin. A veritable rebuke to cholesterol. Free of hormones and antibiotics. Good with Calvados sauce say the gourmets.

But like all good conversations ours moved on to... sex. The big question. How to tell male from female? Not to mention possibilities of bi- or trans-sexuality. Flightless it may be, but what was the right technique to get close enough to work out the operative gender? My informant spoke darkly of ropes, lassoes, teams of farmhands with clasped arms. You might also get kicked in places you wouldn't want to be or rammed by the one or another enraged *struthio*.

But once you have the bird pinioned then it's a question of biological fine art.

Sexing. Gender assignment. The which of the usual two.

Apparently this entails some delicate, shall we say, handling. In you plunge. Or rather in plunges your mitt. Through a corridor of feathers. The ostrich itself usually lets out squawks like the sound of a banshee. Wings try to beat with the force of a typhoon. The neck gyrates as though whiplash were its middle name.

Meantime the hand goes about its work. Genital search and report. And if not with quite a cry of Eureka your sex-determiner pronounces.

It is not, apparently, a job that has thousands applying.

Mainly seasoned ostrich-farm Oklahomans.

But also occasionally people with a twitch.

RACING PARROT

It's no good. I just can't keep my eyes off those Nature documentaries. *Winter in Wild Siberia. Summer Patagonia. Spring Barrier Reef.*

Plus the animals. Wolves in Alaska. Manatees in the Everglades. Blue footed boobies in the Galápagos. Giant lobsters off the Maine Coast. Herds of blue-seeming Wildebeests defying (or not) crocodiles in the Serengeti. Lone basking sharks. And that shared favourite – the Kalahari meerkat.

Whichever features, predator or prey, wing or fin, I'm hooked. Or rather not so much hooked but locked into comfort viewing. No complex plots. No need to try to remember this actor, that locale. I've even found myself watching ant raids, tapir motherhood, python jaw reflexes, hammerhead shark hunting skills, and hyena pack behaviour. Along with octopus reproduction.

Nor can it be said that any one preference rules. But I confess to an especial liking for those shots, the swoop, perch or landing, of multihued birds. Your flock of pink-red landing flamingo. Your don't-give-a-snoot Indian peafowl with its blue crest and neck. Your white storks nested in Belgian rooftop chimneys.

That includes any number of Amazon vistas. Seriously billed yellow and black toucans. Fanned hoatzin. Magisterial harpy eagles.

Above all, parrots. A whole profusion of kinds and species. Not least the stark green and unfussily named

Amazon Parrot itself. Go to other river and jungle venues and you are into feather-colour parrot heaven: red-blue, scarlet, love-bird tangerine, soft turquoise.

In a move to full-time residence in Spain I little thought this avian repertoire would have undue bearing. The usual starlings and sparrows. A maybe hawk if you were up in the hills. Morning larks. A grebe or two. The occasional city river heron.

Imagine, then, a morning whose night-before had even been early to bed and without any intake of *vino tinto*, or for that matter *vino blanco*. This was the morning that my eyes alighted on a FLYING PARROT.

Could the back porch have become some landing site for one of Brazil's or the Congo's feathered best? Had I finally just seen too many documentaries and was in the grip of pixel hallucination? Was I witness to a jail-break, or rather a birdcage-break? Thoughts came to mind of over-the-wall escapees, some bird equivalent of tunnel diggers. Quite why I'm not sure, there was passing remembrance of the Birdman of Alcatraz. Robert Stroud played, quite against history, by a gentle, humane Burt Lancaster in the film of 1962.

Either way, there it was. In living colour. Bona fide quills. Flapping wings. An antenna of a beak. Feet astride the air and in descent mode ready for the rear porch touch-down.

Duly it landed. Duly it started to strut. Head bobbing up and down.

But whether it was the intake of a cup of mocha or some wiping of my specs, I began to suspect something was not quite right. Did parrots really bob like that? And that coo-sound, surely not the phonetics of a parrot?

So into Sherlock ornithology mode.

Damn. No. Damn and damn again. This was an imposter. A fake. A double dealer. Not quite some gilded lily but whatever the bird equivalent is of a trickster.

These were painted feathers. The neck was one colour, the body a garish melee of others. Cheap rainbow as it became apparent once you got closer.

Then it began to dawn.

What we were dealing with here was... a Spanish racing pigeon. *Una paloma al aire*. Locals keep them in rows of dovecots (though I never hear them called pigeoncots). Neon bird sprinters.

A village man I know explained that the procedure is to release a female and then have a pigeon rugby scrum of males wing after her. A love chase. The paint is to distinguish the different teams. It is a sports *especialidad* of 'my' part of Spain. The Iberian southeast of Murcia and Valencia.

This particular errant male now took up residence atop next door's air conditioning unit. Maybe the vibrations. Maybe it thought it was the discovery of a new home. Maybe a sex hum.

It would then take to swooping into our porch. A pause at this shrub. A peck at that passing ant. The up and down neck movements that went with every forward step.

Not so much colour-coordinated as living colour-spectrum.

Obviously a *flâneur*. Too much Baudelaire, not to mention Julian Barnes, if you ask me.

A pigeon above its station.

A popinjay.

And yours truly looking on as though at a 3D movie.

THE GOD PARTICLE

A trip to the visiting Fair just as I was launched into
teenagery was almost de rigueur. Off you clattered,
usually a bunch of you. Boys. Lots of clanging music.
Shouts.

Ahead lay dodgems, a rifle range, a rickety haunted
house if you were lucky, and merry go rounds which
I had not yet learned to call carousels. These, of
course, were unworthy of your patronage – the fare
of screaming sub-teenagers or, and what a mixture of
disdain and interest was to be attached, girls.

The eye turned to slot machines which, especially after
dark, looked and sounded like Daleks in the making.
Maybe you bought cotton candy floss on a stick, white
or pink, which you tried to eat but which clung to the
lips like sugared fog and always left you with sticky
digits.

You'd come home, all coinage spent, with a one-eyed
bear. Or some supremely useless plastic trinket. On
one occasion, who can say why, I found myself with
a bevel-edged chamber pot. It was given to me by a
discombobulated mother whose pride and joy, three
going on four, was clearly over-tired, screaming, and
with cheeks streaked in tears. The pot has been won in
a small everyone-a-winner tent raffle. But the mother
wanted off and home, her own clearance sale. So it
came, I should say it was thrust, my way.

One booth in particular always drew you. Not the one
with the mini-crane which you paid into and then, like

the slowest death march, was to be so manoeuvred as
to knock a chocolate bar or key ring into the waiting
tray. Not the one festooned with gypsy heads and called
you in to have your palm read, your future foretold.
Not even the one which had a gnarled ex-boxer, nose
akimbo, left eye a notch below his right, with whom
you were enjoined to go three rounds and win a prize
punching stand.

No, I am speaking of the booth with disconsolate-
looking goldfish swimming in circles in their small glass
bowls. As if they had a choice. If you landed a ping-
pong ball in one of these bowls, the goldfish were yours.

It must have been that there was baseball pitcher lurking
in my genes, or some hitherto unrecognised hammer
thrower. But one of the plastic balls somehow scored
and there I was, a fish-handler. Home it came, with a fair
amount of spilling, to be duly given place of honour on
the bedroom window ledge. Peril, however, lay to hand.

How was I to know the true dangers of sunlight? Back I
came from school. And there, like accusing ghosts, were
three belly-up goldfish. Dead as winter leaves.

I was still, about this time, a creature of school religion.
Nominal for sure. Gestural. But habituated to a prayer
or two, occasional hymns. As much simply by locale
and habit a kind of easy-on-the-spirit Anglicanism. The
upshot was that I decided to give my fish a Christian
burial.

Off to the small back garden I trundled. Three little fish.
Three little graves.

Had I even the slightest better inkling of theology
I might have known about Christianity and fish.
ICHTHYS. Greek for fish. Initials that spell out the
religion's founder.

Had my fairground education continued I might have
learned the Tarot and the role of fish as symbols of
emotion.

How was I to know that another fish, a whale, would
have a role in my academic life as I took on literature and
the author of *Moby-Dick*? Even if, strictly, a whale is not
a fish.

Could anyone have predicted that, years still later, mine
would be a life lived in Japan with its reverence for *koi*
and next to the China of *Feng Shui*.

But that was all future tense. For the moment I was in
fish mode. And dimly aware of hymn lines like 'For
Those in Peril on the Sea.' So, the young repentant, I
stood before my own bowl-born cemetery, a mourner of
goldfish eye, tail, the swirls of orange.

It was about an hour later that I heard animal shrieks. As
I looked out the sight was of two cats, fighting. Feline
snarls. Claws out.

And there, strewn like miniscule vertebrae, bone ferns,
were what was left of those valiant if deceased fish.

How, at the time, to have even imagined issues of
transmigration of souls? Plato and metempsychosis?
Or a Donne poem of that name? Or a story by Poe? Or
wordplay by Joyce?

No more life after death. No more souls. No more fish and other theology.

What I was faced with, then and since, was the cat's dinner.

IDEAL PORTUGAL

You could be on a late-night bus. Or find yourself lost in a supermarket aisle and wondering if you said you'd get the courgettes. Which I remember are called zucchini in New York. As, I also remember, they are in the rest of America.

Improbably, but then not, who pops into your mind but... Homer?

And what he has to say about Elysium. Didn't he say that it was somewhere at the Ocean's Edge, an enchanted or perfect place? Which has you dipping into school-time French to see if you can still pronounce Champs Elysées and not sound like Hitler. And isn't there an Elysian Fields Avenue in New Orleans – which you read about in that class on Tennessee Williams's *A Streetcar Named Desire*?

All of which, Greece, France or the USA, is better than worrying about courgettes. Or, since you have remembered, zucchini.

Funny about ideal things.

Or ideal places.

Or ideal people.

Or ideal days out.

Or ideal shoes.

Or, and here's the rub, ideal lunches – though you could make that dinners.

Because there are the thousand conversations you've had about eats. The brasserie that does you an exquisite second course. The country pub that serves quality wine by the glass at a more than reasonable price.

Think of all those 'converted' venues where you have enjoyed wining and dining, and likely over-doing both. Old firehouses. A railway station or two. A crofter's cottage now reworked into upper and lower service. In Seoul I recall being taken for *kimchi* to a place that used to be a truss-maker's.

You likely have a fond but increasingly dim holiday memory of a terrace eatery you found near the sea. Mediterranean fresh-that-morning grilled sardines. A right Macon Blanc. And the complimentary dessert glass of Vin Santo.

You may, of course, have overlaid all this with too many Bogie-Bacall movies. Too many Hollywood twilight dinners. Or you may simply be trying to get your mind off those courgettes.

It was in Spain that I got into ideal lunches. That is the wish for them. I found myself in company that was planning a trip to the north, to Santiago de Compostela. But via Portugal. One of our number knew a restaurant just outside Oporto so breathtakingly good that gourmets might have speeded there in culinary droves. He spoke of *bacalhau na cataplana,* a cod dish almost loved to death in oil, garlic, clams, ham and other gastronomic conspiracy. There was necessary mention of the wines to which Oporto gives its name.

This, however, was a small place, not especially celebrated in any gastronome's must-do list. But if you wanted gustatory heaven, a dining-table palace of delights, there could be little doubt that here was a contender. Palates thus aroused, it was up and off.

All roads to Lusitanian satiety.

Oporto, Porto in Portuguese, came and went. A glimpse of the Douro river. A sighting of the statue of Prince Henry the Navigator – full monicker *Henrique, o navegador*. A dip into the blue-tiled station with the injunction *Por favor —não alimente os pombos*. Don't feed the pigeons. Then we were off for the countryside. A horse or two to be seen. Flights of birds.

And, in due course and like mariners home from the sea, or Patagonian trekkers, we fetched up at our village, our own eatery. The rumble of stomach. Whetted lip. Deft parking of cars. A liveliness of step.

And there, like a message from Gomorrah, was a hand-written sign:

DESCULPE, OBRAS: FECHADO UM MÊS

SORRY, REPAIRS: CLOSED FOR A MONTH

Ideal Portugal was to be on hold. It may be, sometime in the future, there'll be an ideal breakfast in Uzbekistan, ideal late dining in Bora-Bora.

But you keep on keeping an eye, as well as a nose, to the opportunity.

Ideal things, meals included, are rarely perfect.

MY LIFE AS A TERRORIST

Terror. Terrorism.

Serious fare I perfectly recognise.

Fear and Loathing. Fear and Trembling.

Global malaise. Curse of our times.

Could it be doubted?

But like all aspects of *la condition humaine* the antic is
never more than a tic, a twitch, away. Little did I think
I'd risk Guantanamo on account of the date my mother
gave birth in a north of England hospital.

If you're not a US citizen, and are applying to do a
Summer job -- teaching by the Rockies in this case –
then you need a Work Visa. The celebrated J1. Fair
dos. Even if it means a fair bit of on-line industry and
eventually old-time paperwork.

Things had tensed up after 9-11. Homeland Security
entered the lexicon of every news bulletin. A former
Pennsylvania governor had been appointed Director.
Alerts were sounded: luggage, body scans, retina checks.
The State Department needed to be seen to be doing
things, making sure no untoward presence got through
the application process.

First came paperwork from the university involved –
bona fide proof that you were hired, fully certificated for
the classroom. Then there was the visa application form

and your passport, with a due full-face photograph.

All a good two months ahead. All to be sent by mail
to the Consulate. No thought on the Consulate's part
that if you needed your passport in the interim it would
be tough bananas. So make sure there was no family
emergency or a sudden need to go to Borneo or New
Zealand. And pay up. As I was in Tokyo at the time it
was payment in yen.

Preliminaries, even so, all done, it was THE WAIT.

Would the passport duly embossed with your P-I-352
land in the mail box in time?

Things got sweaty, ever more anxious. No passport. No
visa.

Try phoning and it's Kafka time. If this, press 1. If that,
press 2. When an actual voice did emerge it was with the
dire advice: *The only thing you can do is send a fax*. The fax
went off. Silence. Void. Another fax. Same non-upshot.

So off to the Consulate. The morning before the flight
you had booked at some considerable expense.

Past Japanese police carrying Big Sticks and wearing
Bother Boots.

Past the Consulate's revolving security doors, each pane
of which so thick they obviously had been from the
same manufacturer who made Fort Knox. Three marines
hovered. To my own eye obvious veterans of the War of
1812.

Once in, bag checked, pockets frisked, you take a ticket and join others seeking citizenship, accompanying parents, working out marriage arrangements with a US National.

And you sit in front of a half dozen windows whose blinds open and close like some experimental psychology lab device. Eyes among the waiting applicants become fixated. Why has that one closed? Are the officials working to a system? Am I going to get to speak to someone before closing time?

Hours, if not weeks of seatedness as it seemed, and your name is called.

You applied for a JI temporary work visa, said the official. As if, somehow, and as your shirt veritably glistened, you didn't know. *We can't issue it.*

Thoughts raced. Were you on some Enemy Combatant list? Had you been named as an international drug or child trafficker? Was it that long unpaid parking ticket in Chicago?

None of the above.

Then, in God's name, why?

The application form and the university papers were all put in front of you. Your passport, said the voice, says you were born in a year ending in 1. This application says it was a year ending in 7.

Someone in the university office had made a slip of the pen.

Fatuous was my plea to simply change the year. The process would have to start all over again. The Person in Charge came over. Rules ruled. Never mind that a flight would have to be changed. Never mind that students were expecting their class.

The only solution? Go in as a Visitor and start all over again at a US Immigration office. That I did and it was the launch of another story, another set of blinds.

A failed terrorist.

Doomed by a ballpoint.

Doomed by birth.

DIGITALISATION

It must have been when my generation started marrying and invitations came for the reception. At the time it struck me as too early. We were barely past college age, and still mindful of typical ventures like student-discount-trips to Herzegovina or summer work earning quick cash on a dairy milk-production line.

You could go romantic and think of grape picking in Burgundy. Or contemplate signing on for a farm month in the Shetlands. There was also American home-stay: you'd have the chance to loiter several weeks in suburban Wisconsin or coastal Vermont as a way into learning the New World.

But local UK weddings? Of your immediates? It had to be quite the opposite of a bridge too far.

It was at one of these that, amid doilies, small plates, long-stemmed glasses a-fizz with bubbly, small toothpicks packaged in tearable paper, together with folded triangular paper napkins, that I first confronted in any serious way the eats announced as FINGER FOOD.

Crumbs, food droppings, were one aspect of it. There was the juggling of plate and glass. Maybe, too, a miniaturized fork. And all of it while you were making happy talk with the couple's family.

You made culinary choices from the various platters at hand. Rolled salmon sandwich. Curried egg. Artichoke tartlets. Cheese balls. Samosas. Bruschetta. Prosciutto skewers. Presto pinwheels. And always a test to equilibrium – Russian or other species of potato salad.

No doubt about it: it was the closest you'd get to becoming a Picasso acrobat.

Time on there was other eating by finger or hand. Spanish bar food. Sushi before you mastered *hashi*, chopsticks. Kerala *sadya* (right hand only).

So it was something of an analogy when the Computer Age included you. There'd been the transition from pencil to fountain pen to Bic. Then had come the typewriter. An Olivetti portable first, then a clunking Olympia (I never got round to the electric version – which one of my marrying friends did and suffered a literal shock when some wires got fused).

Cometh, next, your own computer.

Screen and keyboard.

Ctrl+Alt+Delete.

Passage of more time and you were past CDs, past Floppies, past even desktops. With computational flourish it was on to Laptops. Each smaller. Each more loaded with options. All presaged the era of App.

At the same time phones were undergoing revolution. Landlines as a term you'd never much use now has its successor in the term Mobile.

You began to hear a changed vocabulary. Softwear. Mac. Word. Tablet. Smartphone. Keypad. Cell. Platform. Ipad. Android. SMS. Whatsapp. Linux. Steve Jobs. Then the late Steve Jobs.

People were ever eyes-down at what, in the earlier
tranches, could not but remind you of shrunken TV
screens, square or oblong eyes.

All around you was text-messaging. Metro travellers
furiously sending the phrase *I'm on the train*. Teenagers
writing love notes. Code-speak like lol, gr8. There's
texting while driving, while walking, while eating,
while in the classroom, while in meetings, while in the
bath. If you have a taste for it, there's also sexting. Body
shots and come-ons.

So, under pressure, you get a Mobile all your own.
Small, compact, an electronic wallet as it were.

You launch. The phone you can manage. A finger touch,
a button pressed, and you're up and talking. Of course
there's been a full body of advice on pricing, recharging,
re-calling, saving messages.

But now it's time to touch-type a message. To invoke
a locution like 'All Thumbs' barely holds. Even as I see
8-year-olds texting with two hands, fingers and thumbs.

For myself it was always hitting the wrong number or
letter. Then the finger managed to hit two at the same
time. How best to erase the mistake? Double jeopardy.
As you in vain tried to use the erase arrow that led to
more erroneous entries. The asterisks piled up. Each of
them wrong.

All around you were texters so dexterous they could fire
off *Don Quixote* in nanoseconds.

You, meantime, dubbed your own digits the equivalent of blabbermouths.

Blabber fingers.

Still wrestling with finger food.

Digital finger food.

WITHOUT

Without so much as a hello or goodbye.

Without.

It's a preposition, if I remember school grammar, when we had to make lists of them, together with sundry unwilling adverbs and adjectives.

One of those words you are always travelling with like a familiar luggage item. Or an old slipper.

Over the years you've learned of some famous withouts. Louis IV may have been *le roi soleil* but he went most of the time without bathing. There were several monarchs, not least Elizabeth I of England, who came and went without issue (I once heard a youngster refer to this as without tissue). Borges and Nabokov saw out their careers without a Nobel Prize. As did Mohandas Gandhi. Wasn't it Stalin, and Mussolini, who acted without scruple?

You yourself have said often enough that this or that celebrity, politician or TV game-show host, is without shame.

It has made a few semi-dramatic entries into most lesser lives. The moment you realized you were without your passport, or keys, or watch, or cash, or swimwear, or mobile (the one with the addresses). The latter leaving you without a clue as to where to go or how to get there.

The passage of time also yields some wry speculations. Imagine, you hear it said, living in a world without anaesthetics. To which you might add without good teeth or without electricity. Would being without penicillin, and at a lesser reach aspirin, be manageable?

Odd snippets come into view. The big-time philanderer snapped without trousers by the paparazzi.

Not that your CV reveals all the withouts your own life has entailed. The too many times you have spoken without thinking. Your occasional being up a creek without a paddle. The failure you feel for having acted without due diligence. The huffs you have shown and left without a backward glance. The Thursday you answered the door without a stitch of clothing.

Of course you might have headed a bit up-market.

There's always been the bard and Italy, more *Romeo and Juliet* — *There is no world without Verona walls.*

And dear old Mark Twain's Huck and the Mississippi —
        You don't know about me, without you have read a
        book by the name of The Adventures of Tom
        Sawyer.

If you are up on Austro-Hungary and Things Viennese
        there's Robert Musil and the three books of
        The Man Without Qualities.

Or you can show off your French and mention *Médicins Sans Frontières.*

Journeyman phrases from 'without hesitation' to 'without further ado', and 'without fail' to 'without a leg to stand on.' You could also wheel on 'without conscience.'

There have been those days without clouds, those nights without sleep.

You have been asked if you are here without your family.

The newspaper is always ready to report someone living without visible means of support, or being left without a penny, or leaving the court without a word, or driving without a licence.

There's long been that sense of Damocles and being resolute or stoic in expressions like 'learning to go without'. Much as you prefer to think this a condition best suited to others.

It also has a variant cousin in 'learning to do without'.

That, in turn, can get quite reflexive.

As in learning to do without... without.

But that may be a bridge too far, a preposition too many.

At least without proper notice.

SHOW THE WORKINGS

A diamond cutter once gave me the privilege of watching how a perfect gem is made. His son and I were student friends and we had gone up to New York's 47th Street, the Diamond District. In a back workshop the both of us saw how specialists in the trade actually cut, trim, polish, and finally bring into being a diamond for ring or necklace. Or simply for display in all its own beauteous colour. Lasers, spinning axles, eye microscopes. Rough-hewn stone magicked into jewel. Everything transition, unselfconscious craft.

Quite elsewhere, in Tokyo, it was my privilege to watch a sushi master. So good you couldn't book at his restaurant for months. Or go there without a Japanese patron. I didn't get to eat but, by chance, it was possible to see through the *noren,* the elegantly decorated doorway blinds. Manual dexterity doesn't cover things. Knife exactitude. Slicing perfection. Balances of texture and colour. Rice and fish made subject to impeccable art. Edible scale. Food as miniature sculpture as though ordained by the gods.

There was also an occasion in Northumbria, England's NE, where I was visiting a local university and during an afternoon-off my hosts took me to a country fair. One feature was 'how to log'. By which was meant how to take a sizable axe and cut down a tree especially selected for the demonstration. Art was all. The manner in which the axe was to be swung with one hand made to slide down the hickory shaft. Where to make the v-cuts. What calculations were best as to where the trunk would fall. Wood wisdom. Eye and hand coordinated. Skill honed through the ages.

In all these encounters the thing that most compelled attention was the effortlessness. Each activity was performed as if there were no visible formula, no conscious technique. Simply unadorned procedure.

And that brought to mind a wholly opposite procedure.

At least in my own case.

SHOW THE WORKINGS.

Mathematics.

I see the phrase, or one or another version of it, has become the very the logo of help-lines like *Maths, Tips for Success*.

Show the workings. How much I would like to have done so.

You know people who can't eat pheasant. Others who can't row. Bicycle-phobes. Spider-haters. Faint-at-the-sight-of-blood sufferers.

Those for whom the thought of swimming underwater means near-death. Those who won't take to the skies by plane.

All of those somehow seemed to combine when, at school-time, the twin gorgons of Algebra and Trigonometry were in town. Others I knew took to them like proverbial ducks to water, keys to locks.

Not I.

I went this way, then that.

In the case of Algebra, which I could readily understand came from Arabic, as does the word Sahara, x did or did not consort with y. Equations and variables threatened. And lurking always was the plague-dog called Quadratic Equation.

In the case of Trigonometry it was angles of triangles. Which to a mathematical dab hand runs close to revelling in an art gallery, getting high in a Jacuzzi. For myself Trig. resembled a building which has collapsed and where there are only jumbled girders and planks. It, too, possessed what I thought was a recessive gene, a malignant spur – all summed up in those *film noir* henchmen, Sine and Cosine. Along with a supporting gang of Tangents and Planes.

Now I am the first to recognize the utter defectiveness on my part. There were stick insects brighter at equations than myself. Children who played skip games could do better. Old ladies with shopping lists for wool could put me to shame.

But the injunction to SHOW THE WORKINGS was the ultimate punishment. It might have been the Devil's Command. I had very little, often no, idea of what I was showing the workings *of.*

Oddly, however, as I went my culpably unmathematical way, I began to see that there might be a way to apology. Some bow of repentance for this show of un-numeracy.

What about showing other workings?

The imagination's, say.

The world's, say.

HIGH ROLLER

Collecting things.

Stamps? Well, everyone in childhood collected them. I especially remember those sizeable Mongolian beauties, all colour and bold picturing.

Dolls? A cousin had whole streets of them. She gave them names, dressed and redressed them, glued them when heads or arms broke off, and peopled her bedroom as though it were a crowded commuter train.

Insects? A boy neighbour had a mini-zoo of them. Spiders were a speciality. But he had ants, centipedes, aphids, a firefly which never seemed to light up, a dormant grasshopper, and a slew of beetles with crystalline black-green colouring.

Knick-knacks? They came later, usually at some adult's house. A cupboard or rickety cabinet piled up with trinkets and trifles. Once I got into dictionary mode I was delighted they could be called gewgaws, baubles, gimcracks, bibelots and more. What stays in the mind are cracks, miniature ceramic fault lines.

On it has gone.

Grown men who collect every toy double-decker bus known to humanity.

Grown women who weep salt tears at their collection of porcelain ponies.

How many times have you got exhilarated if foot-weary
looking at collections of Dutch Masters, or Japanese
sumi-e or African American quilts?

I've seen French viticulturalists turn all Rimbaud
or Mallarmé over their vintage wine collections. A
Singapore oenophile once showed me his highly selective
collection of Australian Shiraz and Grenach.

Not a few times you will have come across a rare-book
dealer who specializes in Gothic terror collections, or
Tennyson in translation, or first edition Agatha Christies.
There are those who collect only books already issued as
Collected Works.

You may have slipped into a Barnes & Noble or W.H.
Smith or Kinokuniya, whether high street or airport,
and picked up John Fowles's *The Collector* with its
butterfly-enthusiast abductor. Terence Stamp would
play the baby-faced and nothing if not prim nutcase in
the 1965 film.

You can dig out a 2009 house-of-horrors movie or
a Marvel Comics supervillain series also called *The
Collector*.

Step back again to childhood and think of those foreign
coins that came your way.

It might be to overegg things to call it a collection. More
likely a small box or bowl of rusted drachmas, a Hong
Kong 20 cents, a silvery Deutsche Mark, a 5 yen with
its hole in the middle, a Canadian ten cent, and assorted
British coins with royal heads on them from a portly
Edward VII onwards.

There might also have been some paper money.

A creased American One Dollar bill.
A 50 rupee note your Uncle brought home from
Bangalore where he has been stationed in World War II.
A Banque de France 10 franc banknote with Berlioz
conducting.
A 50 Kroner Norwegian note.

If you didn't think the term a type of circus performance
or aerobic exercise you have edged your way towards
numismatics.

It wasn't quite that, however, that prepared the way for
my two moments of Big Money experience, paper cash
at its most dangerous.

The first was Spain, early 1960s. We were all nothing
if not pre-the-Euro. My first trip to Iberia. *Paella. Vino
Tinto.* And paper pesetas. Hundreds of them. Sad,
infinitely soiled remnants of commercial transaction.
Touch one and die. On exiting the country there were
Guardia Civil inspectors (Franco was still alive). Were
you carrying more than your allotted quantity out of
the country? Not if you could have called Sir Alexander
Fleming on your behalf. The sight of them was enough
to make penicillin cringe in fear. Even so a tranche had
to be handed over. Yourself an early Carlos Slim or Bill
Gates. With greased cash to prove it.

The second was Poland, 1980s. And paper złotys.
All of them looking like they had been flogged into
submission. I'd been there for a university exchange
right amid the politics of Solidarność. Lech Wałesa
and General Jaruzelski (always in dark glasses). For

the first time in my life I even heard the phrase 'złoty millionaire'. There may have been one, two, hidden behind high walls. Certainly there was no gadarene rush to change anyone's Swiss francs, or Dutch guilders, into złotys. For my part I'd accumulated a fair pile of them. Once again came exit time. Dour militia stood close to Passport Control. And the familiar question: how many were you carrying? Not enough to cause the downfall of the Polish state apparently. I have them still.

Both collections linger.

My ventures into high stakes finance.

My bow into currency flows.

With used bankrolls to prove it.

EX MARKS THE SPOT

Ex-footballers.
Ex-headmistresses.
Ex-bankers.

Just plain ex for a divorced spouse. Yours. Hers. Though
Canadians also use ex for examination.

You can log up a multitude of others.

Ex-members and ex-practitioners.
Ex-listed and ex-directory.

How about the ex-priest or ex-addict?

Or an ex-prisoner like Dickens' Magwitch or Malcolm
X? Did you ever read Dumas's *The Count of Monte Cristo*,
French original of 1844 *Le Compte de Monte Cristo*? Or
was it one of the many screen versions? Which, so you
know, can be seen in Japanese and Turkish versions as
well as those in French and English.

A dash of papal infallibility will give you *ex-cathedra*.
Committees, politics to sports, adopt members *ex-officio*.

The hyphen, it has to be said, is a bit wobbly. Sometimes
there, sometimes not.

Since things have gone Latin how about that heavy
hitter, *ex post facto*, the retroactive action? Or the
legalism, *ex parte*, for one-sided action?

Bookplates, whether printed or ink-penned in cursive
handwriting over the owner's name, vaunt the tag *Ex
Libris*. Which always struck me as not a little redundant.

Other terms have their ex built-in, as it were, part of the
word's furniture.

Guilty parties get exonerated.
Present company gets exempted.
Holiday companies advertise excursions.
Statistics exaggerate.
In a whole variety of ways you engage in examinations.
And you never forget how the French Revolution,
courtesy of Madame Guillotine, did a busy trade in
execution.

If you're feeling a wave of philosophy coming your
way after the third glass of Merlot you might be heard
to utter that everything we do or say is immediately
ex-. That is time as all-consuming, a black hole pulling
everything, even light, into itself.

More terrestrially there's your ex-address. The one that
still gets some of your letters and which friends you
haven't seen in an age still think is the right one.

That, in its own way, connects to another ex-style
phenomenon.

Ex-capitals.

A fair number of them.

Not too long ago, on a visit to Berlin, I saw a sign
in the Reichstag building of the Bundestag saying

THANK YOU BONN. Odd that it was in English. But a reminder of Cold War history, the 1940s Airlift. Here was Bismarck's Prussian capital temporarily sidelined in favour of Bonn, by the Rhine. The Romans left a fort. Beethoven bowed into life there. It's twinned with Tel Aviv. So amid straight roads, glorious music, and a connection to the Holy Land, Bonn has its place. And it's an ex-capital. Or not strictly so. Technically it is called the second capital. Which, by the laws of paradox, is why it gets a first mention.

As to the USA, the country is positively shameless. You may cling to the fond illusion that the capital has all along been Washington DC. But the ex's are legion. Eight of them no less, among them Philadelphia, Baltimore, York, Lancaster, Princeton, Trenton, and New York. You've also got to factor in the other ex's. The Confederate South gave Montgomery, Alabama the boot for Richmond, Virginia. State capitals have come and gone like geography thieves in the night. In the American capital stakes you're kind of nobody if you haven't done a flit.

Step over to Asia and you have Tokyo for Kyoto. Ancient temple domain for postmodern metropolis. That *kyo* in both, meaning East, links them like parent and child.

Grandiosity has its part to play. How not to take note of Brasilia which made old-time Rio an ex? But then Rio itself, if you check the history textbooks, at one point took over from Lisbon as Capital of Greater Portugal when Bonaparte was on the point of invading the peninsula. Who forgets Naypidaw in Myanmar (itself ex-Burma) the secluded ghost-city far from anywhere which gave Yangon/Rangoon the shove? Can Côte d'Ivoire's Yammoussoukro easily be overlooked and which the multisyllabic President Félix Houpouët-Boigny gave the nod to over Abidjan?

Go capital-trawling further and you come up with Sri Lanka's Colombo making way for Sri Jayawardenepu Kotte. Add in The Philippines' Quezon City for a return to Manila; the double ex-ing of Norway's Trondheim and Bergen for Oslo (granted that happened in the eleventh and thirteenth centuries); and Melbourne, first stamped on to Aboriginal territory and named for the 2nd Viscount, for Canberra. Winchester held sway in England until the Normans and 1066 when London with its Thames and Estuary accent took over.

Capitalnostalgie. As Bismarck himself might have said.

How does it affect you if you are an ex-capital? Pangs of displacement or a burden lifted?

Do you ask for map therapy?

Or does it simply get filed under another ex, the one in next?

WON IN TRANSLATION

Bookshops have shelves groaning with them. Tapes, some suspiciously left half-wound, linger in car drawers. You can upload, download, any amount of classes from the internet. TV educational channels advertise them as often as cookery or driving school courses. Dictionaries big and small you purchase with the resolve of a medieval scholar.

Grammars and phrasebooks proliferate. And there are a thousand Academies, Schools, Extra-Mural programmes, together with Open University packages.

I am speaking, of course, about learning a Foreign Language. Long after your schooldays.

Speak like a Native. 15 minutes a day. Three weeks, three months, and you'll be fluent.

New and improved audio system.

Away with those school-time grammar struggles.

Get going! Avanti! Allez-y.

Hola. Konnichiwa. Guten Tag. Ni Hao. Shalom.

Special discounts.

Moments arise under this barrage when you could fancy yourself a UN translator. Or Viktor Sukhodrev, the Russian translator who gave you Kruschchev, Brezhnev and Gorbachev in English. Or one of the Multilinguals who host the Eurovision Song Contest. Or the anthropologist who speaks one of the Amazon or sub-Saharan tongues.

Or even Baudelaire translating Poe.

Or, simply, the person in your group who knows enough holiday Greek to order local moussaka and a bottle of Thessaly *rosé*.

But you could hardly have anticipated so unlikely a source of instruction as Sports Broadcasting. In sports, moreover, familiar or otherwise, that you thought somehow reserved for one language. Largely meaning yours.

You may, as in my own case, have had the good fortune to live much in other countries with their respective languages. You may have made stern efforts to master each or all.

You, too, may have ransacked bookshops, indeed played tapes halfway, tried downloading this or another course. You may even have bent the ear of, if not slightly stunned, that one neighbour from Denmark or Singapore who has to listen as you mangle his/her language before replying in a perfect articulation of your own.

But sport?

It really started for me in Tokyo where I found myself resident for fourteen years. With a TV. And with six-times-a-year broadcast sumo. As the two behemoths set

about each other in the *dohyo,* the fight circle, I learned
to yell staccato-like with the *gyoji* or referee the word
nokotta – you are still in the ring, keep fighting.

Lately it's been German snooker. Players mainly from
the English-speaking world more and more skedaddle to
China as a venue and find themselves under commentary
from voices originating in Hamburg or Munich. *Es ist…
einhundsiebenundvierstigste*! you hear for the maximum
break. *Weisse Kugel,* white ball, indeed lets you know
which ball is being hit.

Spanish residence has you hearing some of the soccer
TV broadcasts. A scoring shot from Messi or Ronaldo or
any other stellar name and your ears veritably ring with
the extended Flamenco uttering of GOOOOOOOAL.
With a hundred exclamation marks following as it were.
It's infinitely more than *goal*. You are listening to a wild
boar hunting cry, a banshee howl, a space-alien shriek.

In Instanbul I once watched Turkish wrestling. Men in
lederhosen. Oiled bodies. Throws. And referee yells of
Tanri'nin adiyla – in God's name. All to do with showing
courage and not falling down.

I remember a French TV sports channel doing an hour-
long broadcast of *pétanque.* When a player, be it some
beret-wearing veteran or some young blood, landed his
boule within a cat's whisker of *le cochonet*, the small jack
which engagingly translates as piglet, you hear *boule
devant* or *boule d'argent*. Both terms indicate you have
thrown well. But it's not French you can assume would
have got you through your school-leaving exams.

It's one thing to think you can more or less fathom a column in *Le Nouvel Observateur*.

But you'd be the first to concede you are not yet ready to dip into the poetry of Goethe or the Arabic of Egypt's Naguib Mahfouz.

Nor are you equipped to try *The Jerusalem Post* in Hebrew.

But sports tongues. They give you a different vibe.

Gymnastics fused with Linguistics.

TV Gymlistics.

Win far more than lose.

Translation guaranteed.

THE CRUNCH

When it comes down to the...

It's... time

Both are sayings with which you're all too familiar.
The gaps almost fill themselves in. Fixed phrases. Word
equations. CRUNCH hits the spot.

The former is your summary of the situation. The point
of no return. The latter a way of announcing the Big
Decision. Zero hour.

It wouldn't be hard to add *In a crunch...* or *I've never
known a crunch like it*.

You also have a bevy of related other usages. There's
always the budget crunch. There's always the person
who knows how to crunch the numbers.

Crunch, Crunching, Crunched. Whole conjugations of
verb forms. Noun lists. A roster of adjectives.

But you also know that there's another common-or-
garden use. Straight out of everyday life. Engine-room
language as it were. Up for deployment on any occasion.
Necessary. Unfussy. Right to the point.

That is CRUNCH – THE SOUND.

Not unconnected to CRUNCH – THE SIGHT.

Sound and sight.

The CRUNCH of gravel. The crunch of certain
breakfast cereals. The crunch of the boxer's uppercut.
The crunch of metal in a car accident. The crunch of an
apple, a biscuit, a carrot. The crunch when you squashed
that old milk carton.

The CRUNCH you see on a Roy Lichtenstein or Jasper
Johns graphic. The crunch you see on an advertisement
for a soft drink, a beverage with zap, fizz, pep.

So it's a word, acoustic or script, that can take you off in
a number of directions.

One of those leads directly to the cinema, the movies.
Pay for your ticket and head into the foyer. Likely you'll
see some large-scale posters for forthcoming attractions.
The latest thriller. A new SF venture. The screen
adaptation of the novel. Cartoons for the kids. A galaxy
of prospective viewing.

But you also will have the olfactory organ come into
play. Isn't this a minimarket? Buckets of popcorn, melted
butter an extra. An unlikely looking frankfurter.

With alongside endless varieties of chocolate, chewy
things, snack bars, tubes of mints, and potato chips.
Crisps if you're British.

There are also all the colas, three sizes. Small. Medium.
Large. Even if the small looks the size of a rain barrel.

It's then ticket shown, off to your seat, lights dimmed,
a slew of commercials using lightning flashes of colour,
and then the Forthcomings, the Trailers. With which full
camera obscura. Your film. Settle in.

Barely have the credits rolled, however, than you hear noises-off. A gargantuan slurp of that cola. A rumble inside the popcorn bucket. The rip of paper carton as the jellymints or chips are reached for. Don't people ever eat at home or at a restaurant?

But then crunch-time. Literal crunch-time. Eargrating crunch-time. Attention diverting crunch-time.

Someone has dropped a plastic cup and, intentionally or otherwise, a foot has landed on it. The sound attacks you like a berserk siren, a *pistolero*'s gunfire.

I've known it even worse. On one occasion it was a Coke or Pepsi can. There was the drop, the slap on the floor. To be followed by the roll – inevitable given the cinema's banked seating. That tinny groan.

Then, God in Heaven, the vain attempt to stop it with the foot once again. Half-successful. But as the leg stretches to infinity and the shoe descends there's an explosion like some minor land-mine.

The crack of thunder. The sound of glass splintering. The landslide. A firecracker.

The earth opening.

The can has buckled, crinkled, turned into a sound chamber in its own right.

Nerves shatter. Heads look every which way to identify the culprit.

And you, the crunch-maniac in question, sink deep into your Row 13 seat.

LEND ME YOUR EARS

You're on the phone.

The mobile. The landline.

And suddenly there's one of those buzzes. Kind of cable phlegm. Rust sound. Maybe the like of a flailing bluebottle or gnat.

You try to muster every listening fibre you can to make out the plaintive question *Can you hear me?*

There is an almost laughable fatuity with which you reply *Barely*, or *Just about*. Or even just *No*. How to say you can't hear to someone you have just heard? It's like saying you don't speak Bulgarian in Bulgarian.

The voice at the other end, moreover, seems to be whispering yet further things for you not to hear. Miniscule verbs. Nouns at long distance. Whole phrases reduced to snippets. Words resemble pinpricks. It's an acoustic smog.

You begin to long for one of those film battleships in which the John Wayne captain says *Now Hear This*.

As if you could.

What, too, at a theatre, or during a recital, when your companion leans and says something in your ear? Except your ear, well, doesn't hear. You can hardly start a whole conversation during the play's vital love moment or a violin vibrato.

There are also all those times that glass gets in the way. I mean a train or bus window. Even a house or office pane. You can see lips moving, an arm gesturing, maybe a finger pointing. You hear a half-shout, a half-name. But for the life of you can't quite make out what's being said.

A shared frustration can be yours when a friend, or someone in the family, starts telling you about what happened last Thursday down the road. An argument among neighbours perhaps. A loudspeaker braying politics or a new supermarket. But, according to what you're being told, the detail had collapsed into a blur. *I could hardly hear it*, you in turn hear.

So it does not come as untoward that the yearly medical includes an ear test.

You have all the other good thing to go through of course. The barium meal, and if you're really lucky, the endoscopy. The drawn blood with a needle that goes slightly askew. The ultrasound during which the gel slithers off your abdomen and causes a mess on your clothing. Not a few examinees get a case of dizziness when being tested for lung capacity and have to blow into a small tube wedged between the teeth. The tube gets embroiled in saliva, causes half-choking, and whoever is being tested finds they've lost breath even before the procedure gets underway. Doctor or nurse patience doesn't take away the feeling of something close to foolishness.

But then come eyes and ears.

The former you are all know-how because you've been going to eye people since you were three. *And the next line?* You read away with those monstrous meta-specs perched on the nose. A new lens is slipped in. *Is that better?*

After which the ears.

The last time I was at a clinic where the full medical card was being gone through the ear-testing had its own cubicle. Not a little like a small-scale broadcasting studio.

Step inside and it feels almost physical silence. A local version of what you think the CERN accelerator must be. Or an anechoic chamber. Certainly it's whatever, and wherever, is meant by sound extraction.

Hanging before you are earphones and a small button ready to be pressed. You get seated. You get the lids nestled around you head. You even see your face reflected in the glass. Cosmonaut X. Chief astronaut Y.

The beginning nod is given to you by the white-coated person in charge.

You have of course been briefed. Press the button when you hear one of the pitches. Each a species of short whine or single bell ring.

Off you go. Concentration. You press at intervals for the length of the pitch. Each of these continues until the sounds get fainter, weaker.

It is here that you can go deeply off-key.

Did you hear a sound or did you not? Are you more and more becoming twitchy, pressing as though so

commanded by some inner-ear *geist*? Are you now so
ear-scrambled that you can't tell sound from silence?
Maybe there's an equivalent of *déjà vu*? Perhaps *déjà
écouté*? Either way there's sweat to the brow, a sinking
sensation.

With which out from the booth you come.

Star-navigator. Yuri Gagarin. Captain Kirk.

Only to hear in quite the loudest of words

I'm afraid you'll have to do that again.

ANIMAL HOUSE

Some people are naturals with the animal world. I remember an old lady calming an Alsatian dog, fangs bared, with a gentle hand gesture. I recall a charging billy-goat stopped by a child waving a rattle in its face. And I still think back to when a small sparrow dive-bombed into a window, got knocked stone cold, and a writer friend warmed it in his palm until it came round and flew off as though all had been a walk in the park.

Not that it always goes right. A burly neighbour who worked nights as a security guard and did his rounds with a mastiff once told me about his animal close encounter when he was still in kindergarten. The class was having a lesson on St. Francis of Assisi – all about taming wolves and preaching to birds – when a feral cat got into the classroom and scared the bejesus out of him and the other children.

My own experiences have been at the lower end of mixed.

TV animal viewing has been one thing.

Vulture legend, imitation parrots and dead goldfish another.

Though watching iguanas snort out salt in the Galápagos was special.

There have been zoos. When a student I went to Regents Park, London, and for the first time saw an elephant urinate. It was akin to Victoria Falls. A Niagara. But

then in Kerala I saw a working log-elephant taken to the
River Perijay by its *mahout* and bathe as though a Bolshoi
ballerina. Beautiful rolls of the body, trunk raised for
spray duty.

Another occasion, in San Diego, there was an ageing
lion, if once a king then coming close to abdication.
It gave out a sound not unlike a dying VW on one of
Germany's autobahns. Sad to hear. It might have been
growl reduced to not much more than throat clearing.

In Shanghai there was a panda that did nothing but lie
splayed on a branch and burp, then defecate, obviously
stuffed, over-stuffed, on bamboo shoots.

It would be wrong, too, not to mention aquariums (or
it is aquaria?). In Monterey Bay, ocean-side and right
next to the Cannery Row of John Steinbeck, there is a
huge one. Gazing into it you ogled luminous jellyfish,
assorted eels, big-tentacled cuttlefish, and anchovies
by the million. Plus a kelp forest. Ribbons of green or
green-yellow. Waving, as it were, in the currents and
oxygen bubbles.

What most knocked me back was one of the ocean's
Grendels, what I half-imagined was a Japanese ghost
corpse-eater known as *jikininki*. I refer to my only up-
close with a Great White Shark. It came right at me.
Or so I thought. Obviously capable of acceleration if it
chose, eyes fixed, body electrical tension. Thickest glass
there may have been between us but that didn't stop me
falling back as though hit by some aquatic pressure wave.
No chance of seeing my name in the audition lists for
Jaws-13.

I can also think of an occasion when, in Amsterdam,
a friend took me to meet a cousin of his. Nice enough
saunter by the *Prinsengracht*, herring sellers to one side,
canal housing with every kind of gable to the other.
All, however, was false comfort. The cousin was... a
python breeder. And there, both indoors and in sheds
with wire netting, lay any number of the coiled reptiles.
'Not venomous' was a catchphrase used. 'Beautiful skin'
another. But, in my own mind's eye, this was to find
yourself in the *Alien* film series. Squeeze. Asphyxiation.
The Big Ingestion. All seemed in prospect. Whatever is
meant by Dutch Courage I didn't have it.

And now to New Mexico.

With friends we were en route by two cars to
Albuquerque and stopped off at the township of Mádrid.
I put the accent in because, unlike Spain's capital, that's
how it is pronounced. To the acoustic bafflement of the
one Spaniard among us.

Time for the proverbial pit-stop. A glance into the local
antique store, everything from tribal beads to aged
farm implements. On to one of the roadside eateries. A
libation. A beer for some, root beer for others.

The Call of Nature. Ladies one way. The men the other.

The facilities for men were round the back via a kind
of patched and woven wooden branch corridor. In you
went. Local pottery urinals. One and another we took
up standing positions.

But just as the flow began we were abruptly made aware
that we were not alone. Over the hedge came two, no

four, ears, a pair of snouts, and the chomp of sideways
moving jaws. There was also a hiss.

It's not your every expectation that while exercising the
uretha you come face to face with a duo of llamas.

Taller than either of us. Full of neck wool. And, we
were to learn, from Peru. No amount of one-handed
shooing (the other hand was engaged), however, and in
English or Spanish, did the trick.

Talk all you will about cashmere. Or an expensive
mohair sweater.

But leave a man in peace, animal-free, when about the
call of the bladder.

In Mádrid or anywhere else.

JUST MISSED IT

That's *you* who just missed it.

The last damned thing you wanted. The luck of a street dog. Jinxed.

How could it have happened? Would you believe it?

You have been pitch-forked, kneed in the groin, punched in the eye. But there's no getting round it. You were plain old-fashioned LATE. Not by much but LATE.

By now you've let loose a volley of obscenities. All of them four-letter. Not enough breath in your outrage for longer variations.

But whether it's expletive deleted or rueful irony (*The Bloody Fates. Calamity Jane*) you were a minute too late, caught out by a whisker. Hard indeed to believe it. A couple of seconds more and you'd, we'd, have made it.

There aren't words to do it justice. The sheer miserable bad luck of it.

One upshot, for sure, is not in doubt. That no holds barred species of being-late athletics.

FUMING.

It's sport in the same roster as blood boiling, attacks of fury. You can add foot-stomping, flinging whatever you are carrying on the floor. Even eyes-closed bitter muttering.

And why?

You know why. Nobody needs to keep reminding you. Nor does it help to know it may not have been entirely your own fault.

Just think of any single one in the roll-call of misses.

Years ago there was the last bus which you managed to see leaving even as you were belting towards the stop. That meant a midnight walk, and of course it started to rain. Plus you had to be up early the following morning. Within a trice you were in conspiracy mode. Had that bus in fact come and gone a minute or so earlier than it should have? But you knew it didn't really matter. It had come. It had gone. And this was the era before mobile phones. Just get walking.

Trains. Not once but several times. You saw it pulling out of the station even as you got to the barrier. Ticket may well have been in hand. The wheels of your suitcase may well have been flying. Yes, this time you could say it wasn't your fault. Well, not entirely. You'd cut things a bit fine but how was anyone to know there'd been a traffic slow-down to fix a ruptured water drain? No remaining direct trains you were told. But you could take a local, change at whatever Junction, and get to your destination either eight hours late or first thing in the morning. It would mean buying another ticket. Just what the doctor ordered.

Gate closed. The airport phrase you'd least want to see as you hurl from luggage inspection, via the deodorants in Duty Free, to your would-be flight. Things haven't been helped by someone standing on the wrong side on the moving walkway. Insouciance itself and jabbering away

on a cell phone. There was no avoiding the fatal words —
there they are on the electronic signboard. Closure. And
you'd thought yourself smart, ahead of the game, by
bringing only carry-on luggage. One of the two airline
personnel about to leave tells you to see if the company
can find you a later flight. As if you didn't know that.
Maybe it would mean a change-at-Schiphol or a wait-
over-at-Dulles. Either way you now have to make phone
calls, talk alternatives. Just what you didn't need.

It doesn't stop there.

Think of that one-off concert, the Bach virtuoso or the
Pink Floyd reunion, which you kept meaning to buy
tickets for and then found either or both were sold out.

Think of the time your best friend's five-year-old had a
birthday and you were supposed to be there, the family
'uncle'. But you forgot or rather didn't remember until it
had come and gone. The child asked where you were.

Call to mind the embarrassment you felt when that
Memorial Service you thought, you were certain, was a
Tuesday turned out to be a Monday.

People speak of near-misses.

But that doesn't quite seem the phrase. They are misses.

Fully fledged. Full bore. 100%.

And you know it.

ARE YOU BEING SERVED?

The Long Drive. No, not golf, but the car. Here to there. Hours of it.

And that means Serious Highway.

The terms all add up to the same Pilgrim's Progress. You could be bowling along any one of the following. Motorway. Federal Highway. Turnpike. Route Nationale. Autobahn.

Your eye, especially if you are driving, alights upon each signpost for distance.

Blue. Green. Occasionally red. Lots of arrows. Miles and kilometres. Major and minor route-ways. But all helping you to imagine time beyond the steering wheel.

If you've still got a huge way to go they can come to resemble water-drip torture, a treadmill. Hours still to go. The distance may be coming down but there's still more wear and tear in prospect.

If you feel you truly are getting closer to your destination they come to resemble a species of road analgesic, highway aspirin.

Of course it's not just the question of distance. There was the truck in front of you that suddenly swerved into an outer lane. How could the driver of the infamous white van be on his mobile with only one hand on the wheel and going at that speed? What, too, the parents who have allowed that child in the red VW to sit in the front? And, OK, OK, you said in contempt at the Mercedes passing you whole shelves over the limit. Your tut-tutting knows few bounds. And there are hours still to go.

There's also the sunglasses. A touch of racer chic you might have thought. But the sun keeps dodging behind the clouds and you half-suspect you're night driving. Certainly the fields all look an odd mud colour and the passing farm buildings have taken on a twilight hue.

Time dawdles on. You feel a twinge in the right shoulder. The leg starts a dull ache, a kind of limb notification. And, to be sure, there's word from the bladder. Nothing if not your very own pressure valve.

Time for a stop.

Time to pull off the road into a service station.

Here, again, you have your choices.

Motorway Service Station in the UK. If it's the USA of car love-affair and Route 66 and its highway cousins, it can be Rest Area, Rest-Stop, Service Plaza. France will give you *Aire de Repos*. Germany does you a compound *Autobahnraststätte*. Japan affords *Michi no eki*, roughly Service or Parking Area. Road plunge into Turkey? Then look out for *dinlenme odasi*.

Fill up, park the car, and head for the café, the restaurant, the shop.

And indeed the facilities. Ladies/Gents, Men/Women. In Spain you don't need to be Castillian to work out *Servicios*.

Nothing, however, beats the euphemism I first saw on
the Pennsylvania Turnpike when the world was young:

COMFORT STATION

It's then on to eats and drinks. The UK does not baulk at
FULL ENGLISH BREAKFAST at 4pm. Plus beans.

Taiwan roads will offer a complete range of noodle
dishes. In Spain there are always *tapas*. France would
order a new round of guillotining were *Steak pommes
frites* not available every hour on the hour. In the States
it's burger time, with toppings high as Olympus,
ketchup and a diet cola handed over in a carton the size
of a West Virginia coal bucket. Once, at a road stop, near
Rotterdam they were selling rolled herrings with a free
glass of Dutch gin.

Legs stretched, lips un-parched, stomach sated, you make
your way back across the forecourt to the car. You can
still hear the slot machines in the playroom. How not
to have seen the trinkets on sale, postcards to dolls, local
pottery, a slew of CDs?

And you see another of the great highway signs.

FULL SERVICE

There comes to mind other fullnesses.

Full Bed and Board. Full Pension. Full rubbish dumps.
Full name and address. Full up. And if your penchant is
for body waxing Full Brazilian.

Also code for prostitution (I'm told).

Full Service.

Doesn't it promise big?

Not just this one road trip but life's every road trip.

ALL IN THE FAMILY

So we are on the footway of San Francisco's Golden Gate Bridge. Heady fare. Suspension cables by the million. Ochre-red paint. In being since 1937. Skyline and Bay a meeting of horizons.

Just a hint of breeze as we set out.

One of our number, an academic ecologist from Brazil, spotted a lone fish traveller in the waters below. Lone and somehow circling. Its snout and tail occasionally became all the more visible by seeming to jump from the surface and then plunge back into full-swim mode.

In no time at all we were ourselves plunging, albeit into conversation rather than natation.

Were we looking at a dolphin or a porpoise? How come it was all alone? Was there some distant pod to which it was making its way?

Maybe it was the height or sway of the bridge. Or oxygen deprivation. Or some affliction known as 'being in California'. But the talk began to turn fantastical, a flight into Lewis Carroll or Edward Lear. Or even John Lennon and his walrus.

A mother porpoise speaks: *Just where have you been all night? Not with that hussy simply because she waggled her fins at you?*

Just like his father, says her sister who never liked the husband. Or at least didn't like him since he made a move on her during a clan reunion off the coast of Guam.

And don't say you've been up-river to that seaweed brew pub, continues the mother.

Typical, rejoins the aunt. *You know that's unsalted water and bad for your lungs.*

And crabs, weighs in the mother again, *you know you're risking your teeth with them. And aqua-dentists don't come cheap, especially if you cracked a back molar. Yes, I know you've got plenty of teeth, whole rows of them. But once one goes the others follow. Look what happened to your grandpa. He bit into that spiny lobster and before you knew it he was all gums and gingivitis.*

You won't like the swordfish drill that dentist just bought, I'm telling you, interjected the aunt, always keen to take a shy at her errant nephew.

Anyway, it was the mother again, *you have that exam you're supposed to be studying for – maritime calculus. How can you expect to get anywhere if you keep these hours? I know you said you wanted to have a gap year in the Pacific, just chilling out round the islands and finding your mojo. But that doesn't put sardines on the seabed. Sooner or later you're going to have to get a job. Whatever happened to the plan of becoming a navigator, working with the human tourists?*

Gone down the river, chimed in the aunt. *Like all his other plans. Joining the Orca police, taking a course in Underwater Public Relations.*

You worry me, his mother couldn't help saying. *Every time we talk about your future you swim off. Did you even bother to send in the forms for that Summer course run by Squid International? I didn't think so.*

Too much time listening to whale clicks if you ask me — the aunt again.

If your father were still around he could have helped. Or at least have had something to say about things. But off he went, too, and is still doing time for shrimp embezzlement. A disgrace to the family. Even his own parents, when they paddle by, won't mention him.

Like father like son, two fins in a pod. It could not have been anyone but the aunt.

And on went this barely-to-be-heard conversation.

Ourselves, meantime, were at risk of some arriving difficulty with our own back and forth talk.

The wind had suddenly got and begun to make the cable tighten and zing.

Down below, even so, it seemed as if the porpoise had cocked an ear in our direction or at least a fin.

Half-overheard words.

Lost in the breeze.

Conversations each at sea.

ROUND THE TRACKS

Remember any of the tracks from *Carousel*, the Rodgers and Hammerstein musical that first made its bow in 1945?

Maybe not. Or maybe not exactly.

But you do know 'You'll Never Walk Alone', one of the ranking torch songs. Vinyl or CD or download you have any amount of choice as to whose version you prefer. Elvis Presley to Patti Labelle. Barry Manilow to Shirley Bassey. It's even available in Japanese with the Tokyo Ska Paradise Orchestra.

But take a breath, a pause. Hasn't carousel turned up elsewhere?

I refer, of course, to the airport. Here we have compounds like luggage carousel. Go into a fuller denomination and you have luggage belt carousel.

Who has not stood by one of those U- or oval-shaped belts? That little square opening at the wall where, on the other side, the cases have been dropped off and now start their welcome journey to your at-the-ready hands? The abrupt mechanical click as the belt gets into motion? Some will have sliding plates of glistening metal. Others do you an old-time rubber beltway.

Either way out trundle suitcases of every size and stripe. Plus sports bags, taped up cartons, skis and surfboards, an occasional clothes-holder, guitars, electrical items to include boomboxes and kitchenware, stuffed giraffes,

boxes which once bore soap powder, folded baby
strollers, occasionally a euphonium.

Out they come in jumbles, antic processions. Sometimes
there's a chute which they whoosh down and hit the
belt rim with a crack that would awaken the dead. And
certainly it's a landing that awakens your misgivings as to
what you have wrapped in your own case.

Travel miscellanies. Proof of random variation.

But then, as time goes on and yours does not make
its appearance, there begins a state of anxiety that can
only be likened to that aroused by delayed vital news or
erectile dysfunction.

Where's your suitcase?

You watch on as eager hands grab their belongings. You
lunge for one that looks yours only to see it isn't. That
one had a red ribbon tied round the handles. Worry
nags.

You can't but note the passing straps that have worked
themselves loose. You spot an identity tag all on its own.
Fragments of plastic pass like ocean flotsam.

Suitcases you have seen begin to re-circle. Are they still
unloading behind the wall? Or is this it?

You know that you are at the right luggage belt because
the passenger with the red hair and that purple blouson
emblazoned with the words KING KONG was on the
same flight and sitting in the opposite aisle.

Could it be that there is a second belt for your flight? In your heart you know better. Not so for a minute.

And then the carousel stops. No, it's not a technical fault. There's you, and three other passengers.

Luggage orphans.

It's been a long flight. Overnight.

Your mind throws up terror-phrases.

Nuclear waste.
Beware of Landmines.
Emergency Operation.

The next, however, has a foreboding all its own.

LOST LUGGAGE.

You wait on in forlorn hope that the deceased belt can by miracled back into life. No miracle workers, however, come to hand. It's going to mean the airline office, the one misnamed Handling Agents.

A plea. An enquiry. A what can have happened? If you go out of the luggage area you realize you can't get back. If there are people waiting for you that will entail rearrangements, killing delays.

Carousel, the musical, could not be further from your mind as you look in accusation at its cousin, the luggage carousel.

And, yes, you feel for sure that the song-sheet lies
through its teeth.

You do walk alone.

Rarely more so.

WRITER QUARTET: BELLOW, BRADBURY-LODGE, GURNAH, YU

I. OGGSFORD COLLEGE WITH SAUL BELLOW

At this time he had no messages for anyone. Nothing. Not a single word.

Remember the closing lines of *Herzog*?

Moses Herzog, Saul Bellow's Hebraic would-be deliverer of commandments. His ambition to speak truth's word yet left with reams of unsent notes and mail. Book-learned. Restless. Yet mind and body as full of pratfall as of Spinoza or Freud. Wonderfully fallible. Sexually not least. And just for a moment at rest.

Not a state you'd really associate with Bellow himself.

Certainly not the writer who won both the Nobel Prize and a Pulitzer the same year of 1976 and managed eighteen or so novels together with a quartet of story-collections. Plus each volume of essays evolving from early leftism to the eventual cultural conservatism that got up a lot of noses even as he was being lauded as America's leading literary edge and Head Chef in the trio of himself, Malamud and Roth.

Certainly not one of the supreme urban novelists *de nos jours*. Chicago as both the Windy City of arctic winter freeze and impossible summer humidity and at the same time a metropolis the emblem of uncertain modernity.

But it was not Chicago where I met him. But Oxford. Oggsford College as Scott Fitzgerald has Meyer

Wolfsheim say of the boy who metamorphoses from Jimmy Gatz into the criminal glamour-figure at the heart of *The Great Gatsby*.

He was in the UK to deliver the Tanner Foundation lectures in 1981, one part to be given in Oxford, the other in Cambridge. A number of British academics with interests in American authorship were especially invited, the reception, and a follow-on session for talk and questions. So it was Oxford handshakes at Linacre College and then, after the niceties, into the fray.

Like many another I had read Bellow with great admiration, early work like *Dangling Man*, *The Victim*, *The Adventures of Augie March*, *Seize the Day*, and *Henderson the Rain King*. Each bears out an observation he made to *Newsweek* in 1975: *I go at things as I have taught myself, free-style*. Be that in riffs on Dostoevsky, the Cold War, anthropology, or Chicago's stoops and eateries.

But I was also wary. During my own times in Chicago I'd heard of his prickliness. Gossip it may have been but a story circulated that, at a gathering to celebrate one of his novels, he had introduced a visiting scholar who had written extensively on his oeuvre with the words *This is X who knows all about me but understands nothing*. Hardly your best diplomatic bouquet.

I also found myself with a more oblique route to Bellow. The sporting life. On several of my year-long stays in Chicago I'd become friends with Joseph Epstein, doyen of America's familiar-essay and longtime editor of *The American Scholar*. He and I, when not about book-talk or lunch or the weather, played weekly racquetball, myself having graduated more than a little uncertainly to the

American game from playing squash in the UK. He, in turn, told me about playing racquetball with Bellow. Fierce bouts of ball-hitting even as Bellow returned from locker-room to apartment to magic the fiction that followed in the footsteps of *Herzog*, typically *Mr. Sammler's Planet* with its Holocaust echoes and alarmist shies at 1960s counterculture, black power and feminism.

One way or another you could say I had been in training for the meet-up. *Herzog*. Chicago. Author reputation. Racquet sport. And as Bellow's writing continued apace so, too, my own reading of his books.

Humbolt's Gift had me doing a review for a US newspaper and remarking how its turns of idea and human ambition magick themselves also into a tribute to Delmore Schwartz, legendary Brooklyn-born intellectual, poet, talker, and author of the fine-grained stories of *In Dreams Begin Responsibilities. To Jerusalem and Back* had signified Israel as a historic multiple of voices, Bellow for all his Canadian birth a historic Jewish American.

In its wake Bellow would write *The Dean's December* through to *Ravelstein,* both novels aimed to take measure of the time in terms increasingly dismayed at the *thinning* as he called it of western culture. The appetitive intelligence, indeed the 'free style' of idea and idiom, were as much in evidence as ever. But the mood was dark, some thought even Spenglerian.

As to the exchanges that followed, the Oxford lecture was a slightly odd, even awkward affair. At one point John Bayley, the critic and spouse-eulogist of *Iris: A Memoir of Irish Murdoch*, looked in, keenly but cautiously I thought.

Bellow was in mixed idiom. He spoke, as everyone expected, in colloquial mode. Fluent. Salted with Chicagoese and a dash of Yiddish. That came with some heavy hitting: Dostoevsky, Hegel, Proust, Flaubert, Conrad, Faulkner, Robbe-Grillet. As in his Nobel Prize lecture he was concerned with *master novelists* (no pc for him), the perennials in an age as he saw it of ever more persuasive trivialization. What he would have said of the World Wide Web which then had still to make its full bow cannot but intrigue. *The present condition* was one of his phrases.

A number of colleagues took umbrage. After all we'd all been to America, relished its proverbial energy, liked much of its art, felt the call of its space, been absorbed by its political theatre from JFK to Civil Rights. And here was one of its literary doyens sounding like some witness to not quite the end of days but the culture's fallen estate.

Questions got spiky, answers had a certain sourness. But this was Bellow. In person. The figure behind the pen. Imperious. Grumpy. Historical. Contemporary.

Somewhat smilingly bemused as it seemed to meet these America-experts.

And they, us, no less bemused about how quite to meet him.

II. BRADBURY-LODGE

Two UK locales.

One. The Mumbles in South Wales. Part of the Gower peninsula. Rounded headlands the philologists tell us may derive from *les mamelles,* breasts, likely so named by French sailors with thoughts of sexual geography.

Two. South England, southeast England if you're being particular, and a Canterbury hospice not a pilgrim's step away from where Joseph Conrad is buried and street-ways with names like Chaucer Close.

Malcolm Bradbury I met (I should really say re-met) in the one, David Lodge I met in the other.

Both of them, novelist-professors. Both of them longstanding friends with each other.

Just to think of either under his writer's hat summons British irony. Twin light satirists. Clever fashioning. Agile prose. Fluency. Nowhere more so than in their signature fiction.

Eating People is Wrong (1959), *a sympathetic comedy* Bradbury called it, was early into the stakes as a campus novel. Professorial pratfalls, liberalism in the mirror. His first novel. Still sharp-eyed as to the 1950s just before the Swinging Sixties.

Changing Places (1975), not a one but a two-campus novel. Rummidge and Euphoria. Birmingham and Berkeley if you must. Each, on Lodge's Preface *the map of a comic world which resembles the one we are standing on*

without exactly corresponding to it. Postindustrial English
Midlands to the West Coast of what sometimes gets
called Berzerkley. You might just about remember
Philip Swallow as the name of the English professorial
exchangee but you really can't step past the name of his
American counterpart – Morris Zapp.

Add in all the other fiction.

Bradbury's *The History Man* (1975), say, with its tilt at
radical sociology as neoMarxist praxis (though in the
case of its hero Howard Kirk hedonist non-praxis).
Or Lodge's *The British Museum is Falling Down* (1965),
say, with its single-day chronology within a London
Catholic marriage and pitched in exuberantly different
styles of narrative voice.

Both Bradbury and Lodge, of course have led writer
lives beyond that of their fiction, each the begetter of a
sizeable compendium of critical scholarship. You could
take your pick, Bradbury's *The Art of British Fiction* (1993)
or the essays in *No, Not Bloomsbury* (1987) or Lodge's
Working with Structuralism (1987) or *The Art of Fiction*
(1992).

But as to our meetings...

In Bradbury's case they were ongoing since we both
had a Big Interest in American literature and culture.

It was precisely an American Studies conference at the
University of Swansea that led into one of my more
Bradburyian shared experiences.

As at most academic conferences the organisers had laid

on a non-academic sidebar. These usually yield a poet's reading, a musical performance. Or a visit to some local landmark.

It was the last of these that came into play. We were to take a bus ride, our guide a lecturer from the university. Small stops at this cottage, that vista, around The Mumbles. A kind of Welsh countryside mini-tour. So it was all aboard the local hired modern charabanc. Single-decker. Welsh-named owners. Williams or Jones, I can't quite recall. Off we motored, myself by chance seated next to Bradbury.

There was this bay, that bay. Heather. Thickets. The nearby RAF training base, once the World War II site of Bomber Command. Singly, or in formation, latest jets soared and then thundered. As our bus, meantime, trundled on in its rounds, fellow passengers and ourselves increasingly became aware that from the back rows a slurred cacophony of foreign voices was to be heard. Then, suddenly, one of these not so much yelled as offered a phonetics that suggested STOP.

Sorting-out was required. It emerged that this was a group of Finnish engineers who had been bound for *another* conference. Also, too, to have been held in Swansea. Much vodka or other Finno-Russian tipple evidently had been taken. Where the likes of us had been re-mulling Faulkner, Toni Morrison, or even the 1920s of Prohibition, they had been all about structural loads, hydraulics, metallurgy. Wrong gathering, Wrong bus. I still hear that characteristic Bradbury chuckle. A page from one of his might-have-been novels. And was not Kingsley Amis's *Lucky Jim* (1954), the daddy of British campus novels, derived from his time teaching at Swansea?

The Lodge meeting was, of course, infinitely more sober. In all senses. A close academic colleague, another specialist in literature, had weakened with cancer and been moved into the hospice. He and Lodge were friends of long standing, Catholic co-religionists in a Protestant country, and to whom Lodge had dedicated one of his novels. It made sense that Lodge and his wife would come to Canterbury for, as it proved, a last encounter between the two of them. It fell to me to collect Lodge and take him to the hospice.

There we had a wait as the patient was receiving treatment. So a chance to talk with Lodge. We made a few perfunctory glides into things literary – his latest writing, a favoured novelist, life for him after leaving academia. But then a rich sliver of information emerged. Since he was based still in the English Midlands it made sense to have some kind of base in London for his frequent meetings, media, publishers, lectures, or simply the culture rounds of the capital.

It was the upshot of this state of things that had me more than a little intrigued. Of all places he, they, had bought a small apartment right above Charing Cross Station. Itself opened in 1864. An Eleanor Cross, so named for Edward I's wife, positioned in front. Trains cross the Thames and head on or back from the Southwest. It sports a Luxury Hotel if you are in the money. Thus as a million commuters hurried in and out there he was – the novelist housed night or day and as occasion demanded at the very hub of human passage.

Maybe T.S. Eliot's *The journey not the arrival matters* applies.

Second home. Overnights.

In its several implications – a place to stay.

Eyrie. Spy Hole. Observation platform for movement, time.

One way or another it seemed just the thing to think about even as we sat soberly in that hospice waiting room.

III. OUT OF AFRICA: ABDULRAZAK GURNAH

Zanzibar.

For years, and in this I'm hardly alone, the name reeked of exotica.

Take your pick.

Zanzibar Chocolate Ice Cream manufactured in Wisconsin. *The Zanzibar Club*, Liverpool, rock and pop music venue. *The Zanzibar Belly Dance Studio* in Chattanooga, Tennessee. *The Zan Zi Bar*, North London restaurant. *ZanzibarMadrid*, arts performance centre. *Zanzibar*, bar and music, in Shibuya, Tokyo.

You might almost think the word was invented to supply the very smell of fantasy.

Necessary, then, to be reminded that its world of real time and place, its name Swahili, likely derived from Persian, and lexically a hinge of 'black' with 'coast'.

This is also to be reminded that it signifies the island off the East Africa coast, mainly Muslim, and carries a compelling history. The trajectory, in this respect, has indeed been nothing if not dramatic. African settlement. Arab slaveholding and trade. Portuguese colonialism. Omani rule. Sultanates. British protectorate. Merger with Tanzania (formerly Tanganyika).

But, assuredly, and quite unexotically, none of this would have been lost on Abdulrazak Gurnah, born there in 1948, novelist. His several personal migrations include a teaching stint at Nigeria's Bayero University Kano and study at London University. By the most telling chance he had arrived in England in 1968, the year of Enoch Powell's infamous 'rivers of blood' harangue at the prospect of immigrant Britain. Gurnah and I became colleagues at the University of Kent at Canterbury – a city that would lend the name of one its thoroughfares to his novel *Pilgrims Way* (1988).

It wasn't every day that you met someone bilingual in Swahili and English or whose fiction gave you an Africa somewhat outside the continent's best-known Anglophone writers like Chinua Achebe, Ayi Kewi Amah, Ben Okri, Chimamanda Ngozi Adichie or Buchi Emecheta or Ama Ata Audoo.

About as usual as thinking of UK pop music in the person of Queen's Freddie Mercury as the Farrokh Bulsara also born in Zanzibar albeit of Gujurati Parsi parents.

Or remembering that the painter Lubaina Himid, British in training and life, was born in Zanzibar which gives its name to one of her most striking Afrocentric canvases (1999).

Much, in Gurnah's company, to learn. Geography and history. Language. Religion. The politics of colonialism and post-colonialism. The human and cross-cultural legacy of the Indian Ocean.

And all of it within the normal wrap of university academia – courses, administration, student essays, the department.

Plus the discussion and mirrors of authorship well
outside Africa, not least from within the UK itself.

Out of Africa, of course, summons Karen Blixen/Isak
Dinesen and her story-memoir of colonial Kenya and its
equation of white landholder and tenant black African.
Granting recognition of the love story, and the style,
Gurnah understandably had misgivings about the text as
a species of European colonial nostalgia.

More to the point has been his own focus. Besides the
ten or so works of fiction that embraces editorship of the
two-volume *Essays on African Writing* and the *Companion
to Salman Rushdie* and the critical work he has published
on a span of writers from Trinidad's V.S. Naipaul to
the South African-born novelist Zoë Wicomb whose
David's Story (2001) vividly explores colour-hierarchy in
Mandela's arriving post-apartheid regime.

In 1995 I put together the essay-collection *Other Britain,
Other British: Contemporary Multicultural Fiction*. One
essay from my hand addressed the after-Empire novels of
Hanif Kureishi, David Dabydeen and Mike Phillips.

Another tackled the then four novels of Abdurazak
Gurnah under the chapter title 'Long Day's Journey'.
Given his ongoing narratives of displacement that
phrasing still seems to me to fit.

For, looking back, I remain infinitely taken with the way
'journey' runs through his writing. It starts with *Memory
of Departure* (1987) in which the protagonist, Hassan
Omar, hears from his teacher, *What about England?
Godless country, but there are opportunities there.* If the novel,
however, remembers Zanzibar's best culture of learning

and garden it also harbours no romance of Mother Africa. In Hassan's travel from the island to Nairobi to India he learns to face the shadows of political and sexual corruption within his own heritage (*We had strutted our miscegenated way through centuries*) and the prospect of an England whose Jane Austen his teacher terms as *hoity-toity big nose and small mouth.*

A similar sharpness of idiom marks out the fiction to follow. *Pilgrim's Way,* the Africa-to-England life of Daud sees a Canterbury of medieval renown yet also the image of racist Britannia. *Dottie* (1990), its ambit reaching from Pathan India to the Antilles, Algeria to *the river of England*, offers a formidable diasporic genealogy yet whose English heroine can also say *I am not a foreigner.* *Paradise* (1994), with its Koranic and East Africa trading echoes, assumes the form almost of a parable: what 'paradise' lies ahead for the boy Yusuf as he negotiates, brutally, African trader laws of supply and demand?

These were the novels Gurnah worked on and published when we inhabited nearby offices. Since then he has shown little slow-down – *Admiring Silence* (1996), with its sardonic take on return from English exile to Zanzibar, through to *Gravel Heart* (2017), with its elegant, contemplative trail of family betrayal within the further axis of Zanzibar and England.

Gurnah has long brought this welcome full menu to the table.

In range of memory. In script. In storytelling.

In person.

IV. CHINA'S DOWN UNDER WITH OUYANG YU

The word 'town' I find, having consulted an Old English specialist, has its genealogy in Anglo-Saxon *tun* or *toun*, though if you're Scandinavian (as was Denmark's English language supremo Otto Jespersen) or German or Dutch you might make competing etymological claims. So, at any rate, stands the relevant scholarship.

Whichever the lineage the word kind of calls up a degree of ancientness, especially of Very Old England. Peasants and their masters. Lots of ploughing. Mud. Cobbled thoroughfares. Marketplaces. Wooden-wheeled ox wagons. Soldiery and swords. And not-infrequent plagues.

So when you get to learn your way around modern-city USA it's always a bit of an adjustment if you're from the Anglo-European side of the Atlantic to hear the word 'town' conjoined to Asia.

Chinatown you of course are ready for – but Manilatown or Koreatown has you thinking. Not to mention a slight shift to Little Hanoi or Little Bombay.

Japantown, San Francisco, is yet one more. Known to Japanese-speakers as Nihonmachi. The Peace Pagoda at the Japan center. Filmore Street. Japanese restaurants and shopping centres, *izakaya* and *konbini*. Advertisements for *sake, sushi, ramen, sashimi, tempura*. It was a touch odder because at the time I lived in Tokyo and here, like a cultural mirror, was its alter-self, Japan in America, American Japan. So that if you bought anything you paid in US dollars as against yen.

And it was there, in all the paradox of a locale named for the Chrysanthemum Kingdom's capital city of Tokyo that I first met China's Down Under writer, Ouyang Yu. Yet another conference and hotel venue.

Chinese upbringing, Australian citizen.

Writer within and across both.

His first time in America. His first West Coast jet-lag.

We were there for a gathering under ISSCO auspices. That is the International Society for the Study of Chinese Overseas founded in 1992 by Wang Ling-chi of Berkeley (where I had taught as Visiting Professor and at many a summer school) and the distinguished historian Wang Gungwu of the University of Singapore and one-time Vice-Chancellor of Hong Kong University. *Home is Not Here* (2018), his autobiography, gives a doyen's account of a huge multicultural Asian and Australian life.

In Ouyang Yu's case he had just published his first novel *The Eastern Slope Chronicle* (2002), a wry and at times raucous narrative of his protagonist's transition from village China to the city that vaunted the label 'Marvellous Melbourne'. An autofiction we might now call it. Reflexive. Nobody's fool writing with shies at both Chinese and Australian cultural fault line and delusions.

That first meeting had us doing a kind of cultural square dance of riffs and jokery. Australia. China, Japan. And, as his eyes saw San Francisco and his ear tuned into fulltime American English, the USA.

Just occasionally he remembered I was originally from none of these. So English irony came into play only as extra-planetary language. But then, as he explained, his regional Mandarin did much the same in Chinese. So there were, Chinese in Australia, British in Japan, and the both of us being hosted in an American State likely named for Queen Califia, a name itself of Arab provenance for a legendary tribe of black warrior women and passed into Spanish as California with, here we were, its very own Japantown. Not bad.

There was a fair bit of life to unpack.

Ouyang's arrival in Australia in 1991, studies at LaTrobe, poetry like *Moon Over Melbourne* (1995) and ongoing translations from Germaine Greer to David Malouf. Prizes.

Our subsequent meetings veered into the cybernetic. Emails. Resolves upon more encounters. But Japantown was it – literary symposia to window-gazing at Japanese menus. Comparisons of Chinese and Japan eating manners. The shadows of war history. Oz as against Yankee Doodle. He keeps being told he's an angry poet-writer, full of discontent. That so misses the mark. Of course he's angry – the overlapping rivers of western Sinophobia and Chinese Occidentalism, Iraq, wealth inequality. But then he is that rare bird, the custodian of an imagination always his own. And from cross-terrains of place, politics, language.

To have met, in California as a kind of mid-way point, was my East-West good fortune.

And on he and his work have continued. Winningly-named fiction like *Diary of a Naked Official* (2014) with its parable of Chinese erotica and money-finagling. Essay work like *On the Smell of an Oily Rag: Speaking English, Thinking Chinese, Living Australian* (2008) which covers his own self-waterfront. Recent verse collections carry titles like *Self-Translation* (2013) and *Fainting with Freedom* (2015).

The sequence he calls 'Nine Poems', published in the journal *Jacket* in 2006, each has a title beginning with the words, *Listening to…*. The Last of them, 'Listening to the Chinese Audience', ends with lines in which the poet recalls being reprimanded *by this Chinese woman* at a Sydney reading for not writing *to make us feel better* and for his *abusive language*. His wry riposte speaks of his own kind of light as against her dark tirade.

This same excavating light, uncompromisingly delivered across continents to two shadowed worlds, has been nothing if not Ouyang Wu's forte.

A plus to have on hand.

VIDEO CONFERENCE

Recorded at Cyst University. Dubai Extension.
Interviewer Dean Roberta Eel.
Engineer Harvey (now Celeste) Graff.

I Welcome Mr. Milton. Let me say at the outset that
our search committee is pretty impressed with your
publications. We are going to have to disregard the ones
you wrote in Latin, though our Dr. Moyst who recently
spent three weeks at a health farm just outside Juan-
les-Pins where they mainly spoke a foreign language
has agreed to look them over. Our main worry is the
research project for which you are currently hoping to
get funds. You say you want to write a poem justifying
the ways of God to Man. Let me be blunt: we were
actually looking to find someone who could teach
punctuation and strategic paragraphing. You also say you
think the fact that Heroic Couplets have fallen out of
use is one of the reasons we live among skateboards and
lightweight headphones. That may not play well with
our students, many of whom already lament the absence
of courses in Skateboard Handstanding. Not to mention
undergraduate library work in gangsta rap.

Yes, please send the reprint of your other writing.
Areopagitica? How did you say you spell that?

II Could you turn down your audio a little Ms.
Dickinson. Yes, I agree, it's right-on music. But 'Born
in the USA' isn't perhaps the best background to be
discussing your application. Your letter says you are
keen to bring more cemeteries, birds, insects – especially
butterflies – and stormy weather into the lives of
students. You don't feel that might be a touch off their

beaten track? Not to say depressing. Most of them are just over eighteen after all and will have bought tee-shirts and ring-binders at the college store. Also, and as you know, ours is a college with a religious foundation. There seems to be a bit of a query about Jesus and the Soul in what you have sent us. I do hope that doesn't mean that you have been tempted into what I hear the smart money is calling relativism or, Heaven forbid, doubt that we are destined for the Great Afterlife? And it may seem a small thing but here where we value good English there is the question of your punctuation. You seem prone to dashes. The college secretary has cast an eye over these and is wondering if they are en-dashes or em-dashes. Could you clear this up for us?

Now about travelling from Amherst to Dubai.

We can manage a once a year Economy Class round ticket.

But our Finance Department holds the line at weekly flights from Logan Airport.

III Thank you for coming back to us Mr. Budd. Am I right to think you are of the opinion that your Navy career will be of help if you come to us as an Assistant Professor? You insist that the 'unfortunate' incident at Bellipotent College is well behind you. I want to be frank: taking a swing at the departmental Chair, Dr. Claggart, was indeed not acceptable behaviour even if he did accuse you of ganging up with others to plot the purchase of a new shredder. It is perhaps not irrelevant to remind you that the blow you delivered to his head was, well, pretty lethal. The rehab you refer to, and the classes you took in rope-making, we agree, are not to be disregarded. But your offer of a Martial Arts minor for Sophomores lies somewhat outside the present job requirement. When, too, you say you'll come sailing by, the committee takes that as an example of the humour mentioned in Professor Vere's letter of recommendation.

Please don't get agitated Mr. Budd.

That's not a fist is it?

I think he has hit the screen – something about Sk...Sk... Skype.

IV Ms. Bloom, are we getting through? Yes. You said Yes? Excellent. Let's get straight down to things. You say you are interested in a spousal hire? But also a threesome? With your husband and also this young man Stephen Dedalus. He, you say, could also be a joint-appointment with History. The medical setbacks you mention, nightmares and the like, he has now recovered from – and says he has never felt more awake. You mention also your ability in Spanish and the flower studies you did in Andalucia. I have to say, in all honesty, there may not be a lot of call for that. As with other candidates we are anxious to have someone, and I'm not sure Mr. Bloom or Mr. Dedalus would be quite what we had in mind, who can teach sentence-structure. Yours, at least in the 8-page application you have sent, seems to be pretty over-length. We also have to think about how word of your living arrangements might affect some of our more vulnerable students. They are simply not used to Dublin ways and what you call Irish streams of consciousness.

Professor Tick of our Geography department has been consulted.

She says she can locate no river of that name.

AFTERWORD

I'd like to imagine that most of the events summoned here in some way did happen.

Actually or not.

Or almost.

For certain they lie behind these various queries and riffs.

It's the suspicion that circumstances are all around you.

The suspicion that they really are.

You have to ask what, exactly.

WHAT?

PROLOGUE

What!

What?

Que?

Quoi?

Was?

Welche?

Nani?

Shénme?

She knows wot's wot, she does.
— Charles Dickens, *Pickwick Papers*

WHAT'S WHAT

What, you may ask on a rainy-grey Thursday and having drifted into nothing better to do, is WHAT?

What, the grammarians assure us, that is the what you come across all the time, is a 'determiner'. Like its cousin which.

So in theory you can easily mug up when to use what and when to use which. In my school-time I remember interrogative pronouns came into the fray, along with that outrigger whom and its Sabbath-best version whomever. Although, come to think of it, some of them may have worn a hat called subjective pronouns.

There's also whatever. That used to be easy. Whatever happens. Whatever the day.

But of late it's graduated into a kind of California sling-back phrase.

She: *I'll never speak to you again.* He: *Whatever.*

As to what and which it turns out there's a fair bit of overlap, even confusion.

Is what day more right than... which day? Is which book more right than... what book? Or is it a case of Even Stevens, itself a phrase of uncertain origin? Although you can learn from a handy etymological dictionary that Steven (or Stephen) was once slang for money.

126

Your local linguistics boff will be glad to give you a shelf of guidelines about context as to whether, or when, what or which best suits. But I wouldn't want to be a Tibetan or Papua New Guinean learning the intricacies of each usage.

These grammar issues, however seemingly so full of point, in fact are sublimely irrelevant to the present undertaking.

The what of immediate concern, and even its cousin the which, point to matters of a quite different order.

They abut upon fare that causes you to react with, precisely, a what. It might be hearing of an event that has you blinking with surprise. Thus *point d'exclamation* as the French say. Or it might be an event, a run of circumstances, that has you full of question. *Signo de interrogación* as they say in Spain, not to mention in Las Américas.

Often enough it has to do with the feeling of being snookered as the British have been heard to utter (albeit that their North American cousins might opt for something like 'behind the eight ball').

You did what! Exclamations.
What did you say happened? Queries.

But it's *whatness* that beckons. The very what of things, lives, feelings.

You think of it in your own life.

Then you are aroused by a poem, a picture, a novel.

You can hear a touch of it when Ella Fitzgerald sings
What is this thing called love?

Probings.

A step towards fundamentals.

Molecules. Time. Consciousness.

You.

As it were.

A kind of what's what.

THE BARD

To be, or not to be – that is the question;
Whether 'tis nobler in the mind to suffer
The slings and arrows of outrageous fortune,
Or to take arms against a sea of troubles,
And by opposing end them?

You get no prizes for recognizing this choice cut.

Hamlet, for God's sake. Want to be a stickler? Then Act 3
Scene 1.

The most famous lines in Eng. Lit. If you haven't heard
them or muttered them it must be because you live in
a bunker or listen to 24-hour pop in giant headphones.
Tins as they are called.

It's long been habit to give those opening two-
letter words show and tell – school classroom, mid-
conversation, jokey aside.

If you're in serious mode, *au grand sérieux*, then it's on
with the philosophy. What's the essence of things?
What's the implication of that double infinitive – to... or
not to...? Something, at the very least, well beyond mere
grammar.

Being and non-being. Life as against death.

There's not a thinker in history who hasn't had a crack at
it. Socrates, Heidegger, Sartre.

Greek thought. French existentialism. German
phenomenology.

And I've held back from mentioning ontology.

You could even wheel on Burt Bacharach and his Alfie's 'What's It All About?'

Your literary writers haven't missed a chance, a trick, either. Flaubert gives over Emma to the call of romance yet also ennui and arsenic. Tolstoy has Anna follow her heart but throws her under a Moscow train. What is death in life, life in death?

You read *Hamlet*, watch it acted out on stage, see the film. And always you've got Hamlet, the Prince himself of somewhere called Denmark (or at least Elsinore) in your ear. Antic wit, asides to the court or his family or his college pals. Above all the soliloquies.

Speaking from inside his mind to yours. One to one, as it were, asking about whatness.

Throw in Hamlet Sr's ghost, doomed Ophelia, tottering Polonius, poisonous Claudius, marriage-bed Gertrude. Each with their speaking parts.

Throw in Rosencrantz and Guildenstern, whether Shakespeare's or those summoned by Tom Stoppard. Asides personified.

Throw in the play within a play. All that shadow speech.

Throw in all those bodies at the end. The one and several death speeches.

But you're still left with the Big Question. To... you know what. Or not to... you know what.

It's the question of, well, the question. Or, precisely, of that – or what – is the question.

It's everywhere. A Spanish TV commercial has an Insurance Company plug itself with the line *To be or not to be with Mutua* (*Ser or no ser con Mutua*).

For my own part I've long had a thing about another bit of *To be or not to be*.

To do with *'tis*. Yes, for sure, abbreviation. A speed locution. Better, in the context, than the full works of *it is*. Which, almost, risks sounding overweight.

What, I'd ask the Bard if we were in casual chat, prompted him to use *'tis*. I mean everyone understands it's shorthand. But given the heavy-duty fare about being and non-being etc., is there not – isn't there – a touch of secret code at work? Does there not, or should it be doesn't there, lurk a hint about all that fare of, once again, being and non-being. Of... what.

It is. *'tis*.

It is not. *'tisn't*.

Whatever. Even whichever.

Does not *'tis*, or its converse, have something to do with what Shakespeare had in mind in *Hamlet*?

Even, in fact, what the play is all about?

What, just maybe, it means.

WHAT, WHAT IF, WHAT IFS

What
What a surprise!
What can I say?

I'm afraid it's not what we thought it was.
What!
We're not going to be able to keep you on.
What!
The drains are still not functioning.
What!
You're not anywhere near where you're going.
What!

The diagnosis is far from conclusive.
What kind of diagnosis is that?

There's another error in your account.
What, again?

The DNA test proves you are the father.
What test?

Your hearing is seriously impaired.
What did you say?

What If
What if everybody did that!
What if they did?

What if that happened when you weren't there!
What if I had been there?

What if it's true!
What if it's not?

What Ifs
What if it rains and if there's a cancellation?
What if they say they are going to be late and then if
we have to go get them?
What if they are elected and if we have to put up
with their policies?

What
What if
What ifs

Exclamations.
A positing.
Doubts.

You might think yourself threadbare without them.

WHAT DO YOU MEAN?

Years ago, student-time, one required text in the curriculum was *The Meaning of Meaning*. Written in 1923. Ogden and Richards. Landmark work. The fare of philosophy, semantics, and ways into literary language. But, at 20, and even underway with a degree in literature, a tough read. And I still had ahead of me the reading of both *Paradise Lost* and *Ulysses*.

A little digging established that it came out the year of Pancho Villa's assassination. The same year, too, that Louis Armstrong recorded 'Chimes Blues' with King Oliver's orchestra. Not to mention Tokyo's Great Kantō Earthquake and Walt Disney founding his studio.

You could even dally over 1923 as one date in the Gregorian calendar. In the Korean calendar it was 4356, in the Byzantine calendar 7431-2.

So how to link all these random items into any one shared ribbon of meaning? They half link and half don't.

Which gets me to a number of recent encounters, language snippets. Mainly from travel. Any number of them I have pondered with a mix of wonderment and secret pleasure. Melting pots, even mixing bowls, of meaning.

Web page news heading: *I married my sperm donor.*

TV reportage of the Argentinian Pope: *He's fluent in Spanish.*

Wine ad for Sauvignon: *Food friendly.*

Neighbour on her window plants: *I was hoping they would die before I came back.*

Flight magazine describing Aldi store: *Supermarket postmodern.*

Promotion of Nebraska: *We cover a lot of ground in food innovation.*

Overheard aerobics instructor: *Now for the warm-down.*

Weekend newspaper headline: *Turtle treated for buoyancy disorder.*

Airline seat-in-front pouch instruction: *Literature Only.*

Sports column: *The new world heavyweight is a raging wardrobe.*

Japan train sign: *Last stop Hiroshima Terminal.*

Golf commentary: *Reasonable swing but his legs are all over the place.*

These, in their turn, take their place alongside two small theatres of meaning that came my way.

The plane was about to land in Asia. In auditory 135 memory was the mantra of *Chicken or fish. We apologise if your first choice is not available.* It was clean-up time. *Trash,* said the flight attendant. The woman next to me looked up stricken. She thought she heard *Crash.* A shriek followed. But this eased when the pilot, all verbal comfort-food, happened to come on the intercom to say that we were beginning our descent and you could get a glimpse of the Japan coastline through the left window.

It was that flight, or perhaps another, when a newspaper paragraph gave new meaning to the mind-body conundrum. A man was reported to have stolen a brain from a medical museum and then put it for sale on eBay. When tracked down he was ordered by a court to acquire either a High School diploma or General Educational Development Certificate.

Can such things be? asked Ambrose Bierce in his story collection of 1893. Or 1300 in the Bengali calendar. Or 5653-4 in the Hebrew Calendar.

What?

Meaning yes and no?

Meaning what?

EYEING ART

So what's your opinion?
Expressionist you kind of murmur.
Maybe early impressionist.
We're talking art-gallery-speak.

What's your best guess?
Modernist, almost postmodern.
There are also the installations.
New Wave or even old New Wave.

What's the best way to approach things?
Whole and parts, design and detail.
You could bring in perspective.
Not to mention thickness of paint.

What about those abstracts?
Blank or near blank canvas.
White with a touch of tawny.
Or more tawny seamed in white.

What about an expert or two?
Dip into Sontag, Berger, Greenberg.
Bone up on Cubism, Fauvism, all the other isms.
Put yourself in the picture.

What helps, what doesn't?
All of it, some of it, a little of it.
Maybe.
The thing is what you think you've seen.

What would you say overall?
A winning show, a bit of a falling-away.

A tour de force, a so-so effort.
Worth the visit though.

That's what I'd say.
Or more or less what I'd say.
At least I think so.
And you?

WHAT'S ON THE MENU?

The meal out.

You've been through this more than once.

How many of you are there? Often enough just the two of you. Though you've been more. Plus the one who just phoned to say they'd be late.

No, sorry, we didn't book.

There will have to be a wait.

How long?

Just as soon as we have a table we'll fit you in.

What's your best guess?

Hard to say, Maybe 30 minutes. Maybe 45. Have a look at the menu. We have specials. Mahi-mahi with the Chef's South Pacific sauce. Char broiled boneless turkey. Orecchiette done with parsley. Our desserts, if you haven't heard, are awesome.

Have a drink in the bar. We'll call you.

Menus.

But even as you ponder your choices, and on the bar stool, you begin to drift.

What else have you known to be on the menu? Other menus.

What's on the menu for you young man? I remember a schoolteacher asking. *You might do well in a bank. Or take a fast-track police career. Hospital administration is worth thinking about.*

It got trickier.

You'd be better off choosing a gluten-free menu.

Try the tasting menu comes to mind from the visit to a first French winery. *Vins de table* right through to *Grands Crus*.

Transition from typewriter to computer brought up phasing like pull-down menu.

Menupages invites you to its website.

The Balkans, you were assured, *have always been a troubling menu.*

Latin American politics? *Yet another mess of a menu* says the expert.

Which, kind of, brings us round to titles of novels:

Breakfast at Tiffany's
The Naked Lunch
Dinner with Buddha

Not to mention off the wall cookbooks:

Last Dinner on the Titanic
Star Trek Cookbook
The Original Road Kill Cookbook

There are also the one-item literary menus:

The Cherry Orchard
The Grapes of Wrath
Clockwork Orange

And films:

The Man Who Came to Dinner
American Pie
Hot Bagels

By this time you've had enough. You're sated. Or nearly so.

So in some desperation, and on discovery that what you thought to order is no longer on the menu – even the mahi-mahi and orrechiette, you find yourself saying *I'll have whatever you recommend.*

Which is what you might have said at the outset.

MEDICAL APPOINTMENT

So you're not sleeping well?
Three o'clock and I'm wide awake.

Were you dreaming before that?
Intensely.

About what?
Being crushed.

Crushed by what?
Not sure.

You mean hemmed in?
Yes, tied down.

Then you wake up?
Suddenly.

Are you unhappy at work?
Don't think so.

And at home?
Seems OK.

Health generally alright?
Generally yes.

Financial worries?
Nothing out of the ordinary.

How's your sex life?
Fair enough.

I'm going to give you some tranquilisers.
Will they help?

They should.
For how long?

A month, maybe more.
What if nothing changes?

Then you'll need another appointment.
We can have another go at what's the matter.

WHAT DO YOU DO?

I'm sure you've said it yourself.

Or had it said to you.

Usually it's a first-off meeting. It could be you're making conversation as your partner bowls into animated linkage with an old friend and you're there facing her partner. You want to be the good companion, not let an awkwardness arise. So you ask the question. Or, indeed, it's asked of you. Kind of good manners. Filling in.

It might occur during a long-haul flight or other journey. Pleasantries have been exchanged. Clearly there's a platform for more. You feel you have permission.

So the question gets put.

What do you do?

Of course it can be an authentic surge of curiosity. You have just met someone who has a complex technical job description. Quite out of the ordinary. Intriguing. Almost a mystery.

It's been my good fortune, or at least my unexpected fortune, to hear a gallery of responses whether I or someone else was doing the asking. Highlights have been not a few:

I'm working at the moment as a condom-tester.
I'm a cemetery gardener.

I'm a timekeeper at wrestling tourneys.
I give workshops for taxidermy.
I offer wax servicing including Full Brazilian.
I'm working part-time at the Employment Bureau.
I play the French Horn in the Royal Stockholm Philharmonic.
I do symbolic interactionism.

Then there are those ever-augmenting queries, not a few of them contemplative self-queries:

What do you do if you find you paid double what you should have?
What do you do when a corkscrew breaks the wine bottle?
What do you do if confronted with a Florida caiman?
What do you do when you find you're on the wrong plane after lift-off?
What do you do about the neighbour's dog that yaks into the early hours?

Inflections come into the reckoning:

What *do* you do? Said to someone else after the electrician lets you down a third time.
What do *you* do? Said to a gardener as you appeal for help with a wasp infestation.
What do you *do*? Said in exasperation when an offspring again goes into the sulk.

Other occasions edge the question one way or another.

Boredom during a holiday: what is there to do?
Repair to the car: what if anything can be done?
The 80-year old signed up to bungee-jump: what might she do next?
The repeat dinner invitation to old friends: what did we do last time?

The eye operation: why didn't I get that done before?
The blocked course of action: can you do anything for
us?

What do you do?, of course, implies that it will be you
who does the doing. That's not always the case.

When the question is asked or put as a query other
solutions are aired:

I read about an expert who said the answer was Green Coffee
Bean Extract.
You could always have the valve replaced.
Have you tried using one of those ayurvedic treatments?
Either sell the thing or take it to the dump.
Ask for directions once you get there.

Of course, if you have a taste for Things Russian, there
are a couple of same-title texts always to hand:

Nikolai Chernyshevsky, *What is to Be Done* (1883).
Vladimir Lenin, *What is to Be Done: Burning Questions of*
Our Movement (1902).

If neither of these does the trick, nor any of the others,
you may well be on your own.

HONING YOUR TECHNIQUE

I
Try Dalí. Or Charlie Parker.
Try Bessie Smith. Or Picasso.
Technique? You bet.
Though a whole lot more than that.

II
Infancy has to be where it began.
Learning to crawl.
Waddle and walk to follow.
Finally the confident gait.

III
Lace-tying, when did it get easy?
I remember childhood knots.
There were misdone bows.
And snapped laces.

IV
Flossing came rather late for me.
Adepts did it like Olympians.
I hit my eye (or nose), twisted my fingers.
Dracularly I'd have string dangle from teeth.

V
The computer age breezed in.
Soon it was all ctrl-alt-delete.
But then came change of programme.
Cybernetic maze, blocked arteries.

VI

Right and wrong relationships.
You managed this one.
You mismanaged that one.
Do better next time.

VII

Try Matisse. Or Miles Davis.
Try Nina Simone. Or Magritte.
Technique doesn't quite cut it.
A whole lot more does.

NOTHING WHATSOEVER

Incredulity
Was there any kind of explanation?
Nothing whatsoever.

Have you had a reply?
Nothing whatsoever.

What did they do about it?
Nothing whatsoever.

Did you get the refund?
Nothing whatsoever.

Close calls
Are you carrying drugs or any prohibited foodstuffs?
Nothing whatsoever.

Have you had any kind of reaction in the past to this
kind of antibiotic?
Nothing whatsoever.

Do you have anything to add to the statement you made
when you were arrested?
Nothing whatsoever.

Did your last employer say anything about the offshore
tax situation?
Nothing whatsoever.

Blanks
Is there anything left of the old buildings?
Nothing whatsoever.

What do you remember about vector analysis?
Nothing whatsoever.

Do you have any record of your time there?
Nothing whatsoever.

Did anything untoward happen on that occasion?
Nothing whatsoever.

Good whatevers
Did the scan reveal any damage?
Nothing whatsoever.

Bad whatevers
Can anything be done to save the situation?
Nothing whatsoever.

The Daily Round
The car. The engine dies. You are travelling abroad.
Time for the insurance, the local garage. A likely tow.
One last check of the dials. Not so much as a quiver.
Nothing whatsoever.

The leak. It looks as if the new sealant worked. Not like
the material we were using before. No repetition of
water coming through.
Nothing whatsoever.

Perspectives
Never Let Me Go, dystopia, is penned by Ishiguro.
Woody Allen offers a December-May film comedy with
Whatever Works.
J.M. Barrie, or even Michael Jackson, might send you to
Neverland.

Michel Houllebecq's first novel *Extension du domaine de la lutte,* nothing if not dark-funny cheerlessness, is translated as *Whatever.*
Saint Paul warns about *Whatever a Man Soweth...*
Australians speak of parts of Queensland as Never-Never.

So there you are.
Left to your own devices.
Whatever or whatever not they may be.

IN QUOTES

I suppose it begins with misspelling.
GRAMMER was an early lapse.
I had a childhood pal who used to do even better.
GRANMA was one of his.

Then came a connecting roundabout.
What, the iniquitous what, was never absent.
Dialect had that usurped by what.
The man what lived next door.

Time in the university and it all got a bit heady.
Hamlet again.
What a piece of work is man.
What hour now?

Lots of other high stepping.
Milton's *What needs my Shakespeare for his honored bones?*
Maxwell Anderson's *What Price Glory?*
Dickens, blessedly, with *Wot Larks!*

Nor are what-transformations missing.
The *Bhagavad Gita* has Krishna in *whatever way any come to me*.
Hopkins weighs in with *whatever is fickle, freckled*.
Carroll's *Snark* does you a first ever *What-was-his name*.

What you've got is dynasty.
A homestead of pronouns and interrogatives.
Plus offspring.
What, whatever, whatsoever.

And you can put them all in quotes.

WHAT THE?

Some phrases, even half-phrases, stay with you like talismans. Or is that talismen?

Maybe lodged there from childhood. Maybe they originate from inside a given relationship or friendship. Not necessarily the full monty, sometimes the half-phrase. A small mnemonic. A kind of verbal tic.

That, for me, has been the case with *What the?*

I've come to love the hidden likelihood it conveys. It can be at first a light query. It can also be a reaction delivered from the deepest reaches of the thorax. Then, on more than a few occasions, it can signal sheer stupefaction.

Nowhere did the phrase better or earlier install itself for me than in Science Fiction and Horror movies. The Black and White of early viewing and then, as cyber-technology evolved, on into all-the-works digital colour.

Usually said with an accompanying *Oh My God*.

Even when the words aren't actually spoken they hover like shadow braille, invisible writing. You might think it the very poetry of exclamation. If such itself is not too poetic.

The mysterious craft lands. Lights funnel downwards. The screen music does its part – eerie, electronic maybe, the very sound of distant galaxies. It then falls to the passing motorist, the courting young couple, the farmer, the child, even the befuddled town drunk, to utter the immortal phrase *What the?* With which the film is off and running. Before you can take your next mouthful of popcorn the military hoves into view along with the bespectacled scientist and Our Hero. The talk runs to alien life, interstellar spores, invasion. But it's the *What the?* that launches the action. It's the very essence of first encounter, witness to the threat or otherwise of another world.

You can also have the laboratory setting. The hyper-microscope. Your white-gowned boffin, often with a face mask, points to a ribbon of mutating cells or wormlike squigglies. It's again left to the valiant hero or heroine (who in time will save civilization) to utter the required words. His/her reaction, of course, is calculated to anticipate ours: we are in for it, in imminent danger. Plague, the living dead, zombies, bodily transformation, a likely vampire or two.

Another scenario involves possessed children. Demons. Skewed eyes. Voice akin to hellish moan or wolf howl. Mutterings in Ancient Babylonian or like. But then the priest responds to the query *What the?* It's nothing less than Lucifer or one of his maleficent lackeys. Once again you are off and running. Will exorcism do the trick? Is the End of Days upon us?

It would be negligent not to bring in the haunted mansion. Above all stairways that creak. Didn't some member of the family that long inhabited the place disappear? Mysterious circumstances. A lake nearby is covered in swirling mist. A large oak bends in the night wind. You need a face, a latest family member, new to the scene. Then it starts. Noises off. A window clattering. A moment's glimpse of some numinous spirit. It doesn't matter who actually says *What the?* As long as it is said.

Which brings us on to other contexts and occasions.

Mysteries, Sherlock to Miss Marple, always have a chorus of *What the....?* It can be Sergeant Plod who doesn't really have a clue what's going on. It can even be the sleuth him or herself.

War films and stories. There's usually a military planner who does a bit of rumination. What the blazes are they up to? What the chances if we send in a demolition team. Special Forces?

All of these, to be sure, have you seated in the cinema or in front of the television.

But there's also everyday life.

What the hell have you done with the new colander? What the possibility that we can get there in time?

What the instruction manual says is one thing. What the chances are of it not raining I haven't a clue.

But, with genuine relish, you find yourself coming come back to the old familiar.
Poe. Bram Stoker. Stanley Kubrick.

What the chance that we have put her living in the tomb?
What the possibility he belongs to the undead?
What the likelihood these plinths are the very codes of all life?

What the? Don't leave home without it.

WHAT MATTERS IS

This is a *what* that has a variable scale of pluses and
minuses.

Try the stamp of approval:
What matters is that you now feel a lot happier.

Or the congratulation:
What matters is that you have come through with flying colours.

Try the reprimand:
What matters is that you don't ever do that again.

Or the call to arms:
What matters is that you straighten up.

Sometimes it can easily seem that you have been
listening to what matters since you were at the maternal
breast:

Adults told you years ago what matters.
Doctors have cautioned about what matters when
treating a twisted ankle, a fever, your outbreak of hives.
Teachers of geometry led you to what matters when
measuring angles.
Lawyers know from long practice what matters when
you negotiate a mortgage.
Sailing coaches guide you as to what matters when
managing the tiller.
Celebrity chefs advise as to what matters when preparing
cold soup.
Was it not the eye specialist who told you what matters
about conjunctivitis?

So what matters, or what has mattered, or what is likely to matter again, has been around for some considerable time.

Needless to say you yourself have also long been involved with things mattering. That is, at an everyday level.
Sorting out priorities.
Setting the bar.
Choosing the standard.

How to overlook your laying-down-the law that a good mattress always matters?
You can hardly forget saying that getting the right shoe size is what matters.
Think of the occasions, quite a few of them, when you insisted that drinking beer cold was what mattered.
You won't deny that you've always expressed the need to get away from it all at least once a year.
Was it not you who said that hiring a good wet plasterer was what mattered?
You're well known to get fussy about what matters when cooking basmati or wild pecan rice.

There have also been the times when the temptation to wax philosophic, or at least to head in that direction, has taken hold:

What matters is that we get the work/life balance just right.
What matters is that human rights be respected.
What matters is negotiating the line between faith and doubt.

But then back you go to feet on the ground:

What matters is that you don't let the vegetables overcook.
What matters is that you get there by 9pm.
What matters is that you change the batteries at regular intervals.
What matters in that you don't fail the exam.

Now getting a grip on these matters is nothing if not a
considerable learning curve.

There are false steps, deviations.

The trick is not to lose sight of the end in prospect.
You could say that is what matters.
But then, once you get there, it's on to the next stop.
Or is likely to be.
Or should be.

If that's in any way clear.

Fewer miscues.

More sorting-out.

The recognition, without overdoing it, that once again
that is what matters.

QUITE BEYOND BELIEF

You really are going to?
Certainly.
I mean how could anybody...
Not difficult at all.
But...?
No need for any buts.
That's it then?
Certainly is.
No doubts, no ifs?
Not one.
You didn't seem to be so sure.
Things have changed.
So much?
You can never predict.
It's a big decision though.
Aren't they all?
It will mean a shift in things.
That's the point.
So this didn't come about all of a sudden?
Not in the slightest.
Did you ask around?
No need to.
But why?
Sometimes you just know.
Why didn't you say something?
Didn't seem necessary
So you're going ahead?
Sure am.
It's a bold move.
But it had to happen.
No going back then?
Can't see how there would be.

It's so surprising.
Not really.
Your mind's made up?
Count on it.
But how, why?

I just decided what I had to do.

PLACEBO

Get your Latin out.

Placebo – I will please. Kissing cousin to placate.

So there you are. One of those words borrowed from
Rome which gets thrown in when the discussion turns
to this or that medical treatment. Or, actually, non-
treatment.

And albeit that the young child offspring of friends once
told me that Placebo was the capital of Sicily.

A pill. A powder you dissolve. Maybe something akin to
a tincture. But pharmacologically harmless even as you
think it is doing the rounds of helping you recover. A
kind of benign false friend.

You can also find out that in the seventeenth century it
often meant a flatterer or sycophant.

Which, almost, and by way of metaphor, connects to
personal relationships, not to say politics and business.
Don't offer me some placebo. That's another of your
placebos.

What, then, of placebo and its wider seams?

Nothing like a shelf of placebo-inflected clichés to get
you started:

You'll get over it.
There's a silver lining.
What goes around comes around.

You'll have no trouble coping.
Just follow the instructions and you'll be fine.
Think of others in your situation.
It was really a white lie.
It will work out for sure.
There may still be a miracle cure.

Or phrases that edge close to verbal handholding:

Try to calm your nerves.
Lower your expectations.
You'll be fine on the night.
Take consolation that she has gone to a better place.

All these, of course, might come accompanied by some
real analgesics.

Aspirin.
Paracetamol.
Ibuprofen.

Not to mention yet heavier hitters:

Valium.
Prozac.
Sarafem.

But if you are out to treat what ails you, or what you
can best turn to, or what will ease your life, there's no
shortage of runners. A co-lexicon of bromide, pacifier,
relaxant:

Homeopathy
Aromatherapy
Bio-harmonics

Reflexology
Urine therapy
Faith healing

Adherents see a Shining Path to health. Doubters see hokum, less alternative good practice than malpractice. Is what's in play genuine help-at-hand? Or are we talking snake oil, hair tonic?

If you are in further battling mood, of course, you can indeed also bring placebo-ism into debate about Divinity, be it Prayer or Afterlife. What's theologically afoot right in the living present? What's the prospect ahead? Does religion yield the ultimate truth or is it the ultimate placebo?

Whichever way you incline there's no doubting that the placebo has had some fair play in the different kingdoms of life.

Whatever it has managed to do, or whatever it has managed not to do, we have all been pleased at different times to give the placebo playlist a go.

What but Latin lovers of a sort.

RISK

So what's the risk involved?
Quite a lot actually.
You could damage your relationship.
There's the chance of a recurrence of the disease.
The brakes could fail.
You could easily lose your way.
You'd never get insurance for it.
The ladder might break.

What risk are you prepared to take?
I'll still take the cheaper version.
It's a maybe investment but worth the try.
Make the decision now rather than wait around.
Plug it in and see what happens.
Take the second opinion over the first.
Book a flight on stand-by.

Are you saying there's no risk involved?
I'm not saying anything of the kind.
There is but nothing too serious.
There probably is but we have no choice.
You get nowhere if you don't take a chance.
Depends on the weather and the road conditions.
I'd say it's fifty-fifty.

Risk?
It's always involved.

Risk?
None at all.

Risk?
Could be worth taking.

Risk?
You could easily get lost.

Risk?
Insurance doesn't cover everything.

Risk?
I'm willing to risk everything

What doesn't involve risk?
Not a lot actually.

What then?

WHAT LIES BENEATH

Fancy a spot of psycho-mystery?

Not least if it vaunts Harrison Ford and Michelle Pfeiffer in a 2000 *film noir*. With all due appurtenances of hidden murder, ghost faces in the mirror, a dark lake by the house.

Load up on chills, a plot threaded in false turn and suspense.

Shadows.
Screams.
Memory images.
Underwater reeds.

But you don't actually have to hie to the cinema or DVD store to find yourself mulling the title.

There's a fair bit of what lies beneath all about. You can almost trip over it. Or get hit in the face with it.

The remains of the old town over which the new one was built.
The coral reef still thriving despite oil slick pollution.
The metro systems that dip from overground to underground.
The road markings under a heavy snowfall.

But then in truth it begins to get a bit more complicated.
Never least the cat's cradle of personality.

She has always hidden her feelings.

There's more to him than shows.
Don't think for a moment they are all above board.
That one? A real Jekyll and Hyde.

You can head over to discussions of motive. The whys
and wherefores behind (or indeed beneath) a given
decision.

Just think of how it suits their interests to take that course of
action.
In an odd way he is still fighting with his father.
I suspect she feels a debt to society.
Why they behave that way is something to do with local politics.

Don't think it stops there. Who doesn't have a touch of
amateur Freud tucked away up their sleeve?

It's a family that never got over the war.
It's a subtle case of sexual repression.
It's long struck me that the obesity started when the mother died.
It's why he has to over-compensate in everything he does.

You also have to take into consideration matters of the
heart, the pull and push of passion.

She was never able to say how much she felt for him.
I've hidden my feelings for long enough.
Why did you never say anything?
If I told you what I felt for you you'd be amazed.

Of course there remains, always, your own inner
circuitry. What questions, what answers, keep at you?

If only I could get my true feelings out.
I dare hardly confess that even to myself.

I've never properly faced my own insecurities.
I wish I'd been bolder then.

Excavation has a habit of always beckoning.

What lies beneath can sure enough surface.
Even on occasion to what lies above.

TAKING THE PLUNGE

Wouldn't you? Haven't you?

What's life without it you hear said. Often enough by
people who actually don't take too many of them.

But plunge of one kind or another crowds in from every
direction.

The ocean? We just plunged in regardless.
It was quite a plunge to start the business.
Learning Old Croatian was something of a plunge.
His moral credibility has taken a plunge.

What, you ask, about plunges you are unlikely to take?

The invitation to learn bungee-jumping.
The procedure whereby you obtain Swiss citizenship.
The way you might milk a yak in the Siberian winter.
The seminar on silkworm cultivation.
Not to mention, upside-down as it were, the plunge into climbing
the West Face of K2.

What, you might also ask, about those workaday items?

We're going to need the plunger to clear that drain.
Have you seen the online ad for deep-plunge bras?
There's been a dramatic plunge in petrol prices.
Why not plunge in and buy those Asian garden plants?

What, you further ask, about the almost not noticed
plunge phrases?

The neighbours have managed to plunge on regardless.
If the music continues like that there's going to be a plunge for the
exit.
She might just as well plunge a dagger into my heart.
The speaker plunged into yet another rant about gluten.

What, too, about plunge commands?

Just brace yourself and take the plunge.
Look, plunge now or it really will be too late.
Do plunge ahead with your massage-therapy course.
You plunged right in, now plunge right out.

What, it has to be asked, about plunge cuisine?

I just plunged and cooked ostrich steak.
Icing a wedding cake is always a plunge.
Plunge the vegetables into salted hot water.
Pasta? Easy, just twist and plunge.

So, if your earliest plunges were into the swimming
pool, there have been abundant others to keep them
company.

You, that is, or for those you have witnessed.

It's an odd verb. The semantics edge in different
directions at once.

Is plunging somehow lower down the scale than, say,
diving?

Do plungers automatically conjure up duffers,
maladroits?

Can to plunge imply heedlessness or does it conceal a certain bravura?

Is plunging something you think you are prone to or something you'd tell yourself to avoid?

What, would you say, fits?
What most applies?

Take a plunge.

WHAT DID YOU SAY?

Jumps and jolts.
Complete surprise.
Even stupefaction.
Imagine saying a thing like that.

Caught me off guard.
Knocked me out.
Came out of nowhere.
Anything but what I expected.

You've been here often enough.
Disrupted from your usual groove.
Shocked, put out.
Yet, just as likely, made to think again.

It's not quite the earth is flat.
Or there are men on the moon.
Rather it's hearing the reverse of what you thought.
The snap of new insight, the contrasting view.

You can do outrage.
How could anyone think that?
You can get on your hind legs.
You'd have to be insane to think that.

You can reel from the news.
He did what?
She said what?
Have they all gone mad?

But it's the one to one that challenges.
The surprise, the unexpected.

The how could you, or anyone, say so.
Yourself in a spin, corkscrewed.

A kind of spoken face-off.
You and the other.
Until you think again.
It might just be you and yourself speaking.

What did you say?

What?

THANKS

My best thanks to Todd Swift and the editorial team at Eyewear and to the designer Edwin Smet.